CW00429136

TopBants Publishing 2018
TOP BANTS, CLEAN PANTS
First Edition 2018
www.topbantspublishing.co.uk
ISBN: 9781718140769

TOP BANTS, CLEAN PANTS
Top Bants Clean Pants - Survive and Thrive at Uni!

Whether you bought Top Bants Clean Pants or it was a present you now have the essential guide to survive and thrive at uni. We've been there, many of us still are there, and we wish we'd been given this book at the outset!

So here we are, look on us as a bunch of big brothers and sisters. Through Top Bants, Clean Pants, we impart our knowledge, share our mistakes, advise on embracing student life, and support you through your first years at uni.

From dealing with laundry, to budgeting, finding a job, and ingenious tips to make and save money. Advice on shopping and cooking, with our very own student style recipes inside, we make sure you won't go hungry! Hints and tips for surviving Freshers Week, (or perhaps coming out of it feeling slightly healthy). Advice on packing lists, personal safety and as much as we could possibly cram in, as well as our own personal stories just for the bants!

Occasionally there's that one student. The one that everyone despairs of, but we love them all the same! That student is Stephen. A zoology student from Manchester. Stephen is your worst nightmare, and yet your best friend! Everyone needs a Stephen in their lives, but be warned students…

#dontbelikestephen.

From the Editor;

The dedication section of a book typically thanks several people who have been instrumental in its creation.

With Top Bants, where does one start? You are so numerous, with over 500 students over the last 10 years, these guys stand out slightly more, with stories, life events, and experiences to make your parents toes curl! For those we've not mentioned, we've not forgotten you at all, each and every one of you have played a big role in our lives and taught us so much!

To James, Erin, Stephen, Tom, Hannah, Emma W, Marjolijn, Dom, Lillian, Emily, Bethan, Bryan, Megan, Claire, Janelle, Alesha, Alisha, Lauren, Alison, Rey, Niamh, Hannah, Kristen, Melissa, Chloe, Tim, Erin N, Megan, Beth, Alison, Kim, Jackie, Caitlin, Helen, Claire G, Dan, Keiran, Sam, Andy, Harriet, Madeleine, Alex, Chris, Heather, Hannah, Casie, Sarah, Callie, Owen, Sonal, Julia, Phoebe, Sarah, Emma T, Christina, Steph, Kathryn, Jennifer, Chloe, Amy, Nickolay, Dan S, Alexa, Amalia, Bailey, Jiaqui, Michelle P, Matilda, Petra, Sophie G, Sophie Y, Tim, Alissa R, Ed, Nadia, Agatha, Tori, Katie, Andrew, Elliot, Eleanor, Becky, Emma, Nicole, Paula, Bethan, Fi, Ashley, Aurelie, Jack, Simon, Katie, Megan, Kieran, Mike Ava, Georgie, Tinderella (you know who you are), Amelia D, Brittany, Vanessa, Theresa, Ed, Jenny, Jamie, Gregor, Ellie, Ella, Olivier, Camille, Frank, Lucy, Benoit, Kris, Natasha, Hannah G, Becky R, Oliver, Cormac, Aileen, Beth, James, Paddy, Chris, Ben, Emma, Emma S, Hannah S, Katie, Jaclyn, Yui, Derek, Nicole, Kristin, Ali, Clodagh.

Not forgetting the other awesome people who have inspired this book, and my life! Claire Wager, Gillian Coleman, Jen Wallis, Carole Colyer, Alison Terry, and Sue.

An enormous thank you to Zoe Shuttleworth for her awesome cover design.

Finally, to my family, who have put up with the onslaught of literally 100's of students to our home, some arriving late at night, and some simply unannounced! Thanks for putting up with me, and the hours of time I've been locked away with my students and compiling this book!

INDEX

Introduction

Introduction

So, the Top Bants team has created this awesome resource to help you navigate the perils of university. We've worked closely with so many students over the last 10 years, identifying issues they hit, fun things they've learnt and gleaning our top tips to help you not just to survive but flourish.

We finally sat with our top team to compare, compile and edit this book. We have left some areas blank for mum, dad, aunts, uncles, grandparents and best friends to fill out for you with personal notes, top recipes, hints and tips to help you feel as if you're right back at home. We've included a few cut out posters and places for you to keep those all-important notes too!

We know that university is a huge leap into the unknown for you. For sure you'll be feeling excited, but have a certain amount of trepidation and natural fear of the unknown all combined with the thrills of finally being your own independent adult! Our advice is here to assist you in these exciting times!

We speak from experience, this 'adulting' thing is vastly overrated and this compilation of cock up's and must haves, is designed to give you a 'heads up' with all the information required not just to survive your first years away, but to flourish!

There will, of course, be many ups and downs throughout your student life, regardless of how old you are. The key thing to remember is that we all just keep learning! It may surprise you to know that your parents and grandparents weren't perfect. Regardless of whether they went to university or not, they've been out, they've snuck home late, they've run out of money, they've survived on a diet of cookies and ketchup sandwiches at several points in their lives! No matter what you go through in your next few years your parents have probably been there, done that and, possibly, got the T shirt too - though theirs said "Relax". Don't ask!

Parents don't necessarily like to admit their downfalls especially with you their beloved babies (sorry teenagers)! But if there's one thing to bear in mind it's OK to ask for help! Your parents will love it when you come home with your washing, they'll thrive on the odd phone call for a childhood recipe.

They'll expect you to empty out their cupboards of all your favourite ingredients. They'll also pretend they're not expecting this too! When you pop home for weekends, they'll revert to their parental states and ask you where you're off to, who you're with and what time you're coming home. Yes you'll hate it but just play the game and they'll love you even more! If you play your cards right they'll even act as a free taxi service as they'll be glad to see you home safe and sound!

Parents adore it when you ask for advice, whether it be on personal issues, life guidance, or financial advice however, do remember they're not a bottomless money pit. They'll enjoy helping you as much as they can but when they can't, just give them a hug and tell them how much you miss them! They'll love you for it!

And so to this book. Handy tips for getting your washing done, throwing a party at little to no cost, ideas for meals to cook that won't break the bank with super easy to follow recipes, and no bullshit! Hints and tips on saving money, getting free toasters and kettles, and a wealth of other useful nuggets of information to help you survive in style!

Remember, we've all been there; we've all survived it... that's all part of the experience!

Chapter 1

Top Bants and your Social Media Imprint!

Before you start uni, we recommend a complete rehash of your social media.

We know you have all had the talk about how social media can affect, or in fact ruin your lives. However, there are occasions, when you may have acted in a slightly belligerent manner on your social pages, or in response to someone. It may be a throwaway comment, but perhaps it's time to go back in your lives and revisit your pages.

First off, look at your personal pages. Go right back in time, how would people react if they saw your comments. One of the Top Bants team did this recently. He went right back in time to his 14 year old self. We have to admit it was a great exercise, and yes, we did laugh... just a bit. His rabbit phase was super cute, but then we hit on a brief period of his life when he was in "gangster mode". We're delighted to point out that this lasted only a few weeks but, his choice of words and interaction with his "mates at the time" was somewhat indelicate, inappropriate, and not social media savvy.

Remember, your newly found friends will most likely have a stalk of you so, ensure it promotes the kind, responsible person you are now and not the 14 year old wild child you wish you'd never been! Then we found this one... from Stephen!

Stephen ▬▬▬
23 August

Sick of people telling me what to do. I am STE ▬▬
▬▬▬ and I will do what I want, when I want.
If I want to bum around all my life I will do it,
because like I said I am STE▬▬▬. Next
country to visit is Syria and I will do what I
want there too. **#YOLO #SOZNOTSOZ**
#dowhatiwantwheniwant
#▬▬▬▬ilidie #ilovetotravel
#▬▬▬▬

10 comments

👍 50

👍 Like   💬 Comment   ↪ Share

#dontbelikestephen

Securing Your Profiles.

We all had that one friend at school that we didn't really want to be friends with but, for one reason or another, we ended up being best mates on Social Media. We also have that one friend who posts inappropriate comments to our wall after a night out. Perhaps it's time to visit your friends lists and consider your visibility, and maybe change your settings to avoid inappropriate postings.

Your social media friends won't know you've blocked them seeing your feed, and will still be able to see your page, they'll just think you're pretty inactive on social media now.

TOP BANTS TOP TIP

Have you ever Googled yourself? There are ways and means of tracing people through past email addresses and pseudo names. Again, we ran this experiment with one of our team here and cleverly tracked down one of our team who was asking for advice on a forum through a pseudo name she used. Aged 15, she'd been experiencing a tough time at home and had poured her heart out on a forum she considered both private and incognito.

We strongly suggest you Google yourself, and use other search engines too. If you stumble across any problems contact the administrator of the page or site and request it be removed with immediate effect.

Chapter 2

Top Bants Accommodation

Most likely in your first year you're going to be in halls, the Top Bants team think this is a great idea, it's kind of home away from home, without parents checking what time you're in or nagging you to clean up your room.

University is a hugely sociable place to live and study with a bunch of new found friends right on your doorstep! Somehow the idea of you being in halls gives parents a sense of security for you… their little fledglings!

Over the next few months we guarantee you'll make a bunch of random new friends who you want to flat share with in your second year! CHOOSE these flat mates wisely! You may want to go for the party animals, you may want to choose students like you who want to buckle down and study relentlessly in the library, or you may want to choose someone who loves to clean, is great at cooking, and good at organising and budgeting (these are the best kind of flat mates). What is important though is to choose people you like spending time with, avoiding the lazy high maintenance or selfish types.

A reasonable measure is that they take responsibility for themselves, pay their round, are not the ones that end up in tears at the end of every night out, they're the last to gossip and are good all round friends.

Stephen – from the Top Bants team will testify to this! He had a bunch of lad mates one of whom found a perfect house. Stephen (being Stephen) agreed to move into this house without actually checking it out for himself.

On arriving at the beginning of his second year, to his new home, keys in hand, he entered the shared hallway. On the stairs was a (let's just say), incredibly welcoming young lady! By the second flight of stairs, he bumped into a semi-conscious body who later was removed by the police. When he entered his top floor flat, he was thrilled with the fact that he had the penthouse suite, which, indeed turned out to be the attic, with leaking roof, a broken window, and a rat family who had taken residence… IN HIS MATTRESS! Please, whatever you do… #dontbelikestephen!

Despite wanting to take on the first property you see, we advise looking at several, or speaking to some second years to see who's moving and why. Be aware that whilst there are some great apartments and houses for students in well situated areas, and run by wonderful landlords, for every great accommodation story we have had or have come across, we hear of another hideous experience! Your key considerations will be;

- How close is it to your uni? Is it still walkable / cyclable when you are broke?
- How easy is it to get to local bars, and better still to get home safely?
- What cheap supermarkets are a walkable distance?
- Can you park your bike securely on the property?
- Are you able to park a car nearby for free or with a residents permit?

- How warm is it? Try to go on a cold day to work this out!
- How up to date are the electrical appliances and are they included in the price?
- Is there damp? Look for peeled wallpaper on the walls. Look around the windows; is there black mold or lots of condensation?
- Is the bathroom well ventilated? Any mold on the ceiling?
- What's security like? Especially if your bedroom is on the ground floor.
- What security is on the windows? How lockable are they? How easy are they to undo?
- Make sure the windows open easily from the inside, and not so well from the outside.
- Ask what bills are included / excluded in the price and how much are they per month (this will help you to budget)
- Ask the current tenants how warm the house is in winter?
- Is there a garden you have to care for? Great for BBQ's and parties, but could be a real faff too!

TOP BANTS TOP TIP

Start your search earlier rather than later or you choices will be greatly reduced, being late could mean ending up in a bad part of town, a more expensive property or further away incurring travel costs to uni and social events.

Deposits

The deposit is the money you and your housemates pay in advance as a guarantee against unreasonable damage to the property and contents, and to cover unpaid rent owing. However, it's a well-known fact that (not all) but many landlords make a great deal of money every year by withholding the deposit. A number of the Top Bants team have been conned by this, and on several occasions more than once! There are lots of really good landlords out there too but if you do get caught out, it can be expensive. There are a few things you can do to protect yourself against this though.

The typical ways they manage to withhold the deposit are charging for damage, broken furniture and damage to mattresses, sofas, carpet stains, appliances, and they'll take a good £100 off of you if they can for leaving the accommodation unclean! The unscrupulous will take money from you whether it was you that was responsible or not. Another trick is to be late with inventories for the accommodation, or somehow forget to run through an inventory with you in the first place, so watch out for this in advance. Obviously, if you don't have a record of what's there in the first place you cannot prove it wasn't there later on.

Don't be afraid to photo any damage or mess that you see when you move in and email it to the letting agency or landlord ON THE SAME DAY. Otherwise you will find you can be charged for this at the end.

TOP BANTS TOP TIP

Your landlord is not going to throw you out for complaining, you have a tenancy agreement after all and it is normal that new tenants give in a 'snagging' list so, you are within your rights to be up front about the condition of the property on the day you take it over. Leave it for several days when there is a doubt if the problems were there when you took it over then, you will end up paying at the end. Also, ask around, previous tenants, neighbours, agents etc. Good questions include;

- Did they take money from the last tenants' deposit and why?
- Do they answer your calls and repair needs promptly?
- Do you consider them honest and reliable?

Please ensure there are CO_2 and fire alarms, if they're battery powered, do please check these every few weeks to ensure they're working! Check also that if there are fire extinguishers, that they have been checked or replaced recently. They should have a compliance sticker with a date on.

We recommend that in the event of a fire, alert everyone in the property and leave safely by the nearest exit whilst phoning the fire brigade. Don't attempt to be a hero!

Household goods

Check the condition of the fridge, freezer, washing machine and microwave. Ensure they are all in good working order. (As a minimum do this on the first day but preferably with the landlord or letting agent) Ensure you also take photos of any rust, broken trays in the fridge, broken seals on the washing machine. Highlight any problems from the very beginning.

TOP BANTS TOP TIP

Look on trading sites like Gumtree or local 'for sale' Facebook groups where you will find lots of free or nearly free stuff for collection. Our team have had a collective search today and found the following free household items

Zillions of free sofas and sofa beds (always handy when you're having sleepovers)
Free toasters
Free ovens
Free beds
Free wardrobes
Free coffee tables
Free dining tables (and chairs)
Free exercise bikes and rowing machines
Free horse manure (ok perhaps not)
Free shelves
Free house plants
Free curtains, mirrors, bar stools and BAR!!!!
Free hoover
Free wine holder (handy for that free bar)
Free armchairs
Free desk

Free desk lamp
Free guinea pig cage (not that we recommend you get pets whilst at uni)

Whatever you get for free, be sure to take it with you when you leave though as the landlord will probably charge you for removing it after you have left.

Chapter 3

Top Bants on Food -STUDENT STYLE

Let's face it, living on a budget, having to cook for yourself and consider a healthy lifestyle can be really pants considering how many pizzas, kebabs and takeaways there are in the world! Be sure that eating like that will reduce your student loan very quickly and could possibly shorten your life! Budgeting is by far one of the hardest things you'll have to master as a student especially with so much temptation and fast food apps at your fingertips. Similarly, time to cook a good fun, delicious and relatively healthy meal can seem daunting when you haven't had to do it before. Here, we're going to take the struggle out of this for you, ensuring you're happy, mum and dad are impressed, and you're within budget. You can even use your new found skills to make friends and fans!

First of all, the food cupboard of mum and dad is a good source to stock up on the things to store in your cupboard that will last you the full year. They're slightly more expensive to buy but, once you have them in stock you will cut your yearly cooking bill significantly!

You can either hit your food budget or, because they're sensible things, ask mum and dad / grandparents / aunts and uncles for a bit of help, just to get you going.

Things that will be handy;

- Cooking oil (1 litre)
- Stock cubes (vegetable or chicken)
- Lazy garlic, or garlic puree in a tube.

- Marmite (if you like it) or jam or marmalade or peanut butter (or all of them)
- A bag of sugar
- A box of salt
- Washing up liquid!
- Peppercorns, in a grinder
- Tabasco sauce / Worcester sauce, or both.
- Dried medium curry powder x 2 - 4 packets (dried is cheaper, and lasts longer)
- Tomato puree
- 1 packet suet (meat or veggie)
- 1 packet plain flour
- 1 packet self-raising flour
- 1 packet corn flour
- 1 bottle tomato ketchup

Tinned food that would be great to keep in stock
- 4 tins of tomatoes
- 4 tins of tuna
- 4 tins of baked beans
- 4 tins of cooked lentils
- 2 tins of chickpeas
- 2 tins of chicken soup
- 2 tins of condensed tomato soup. If you can run to it, grab 2 tins of chicken or vegetable soup too! They come in handy to make super cheap tasty sauces!

It's always worth chancing one or two luxuries;

- Coffee or tea
- Chocolate milkshake mix for hot chocolate or for baking our famous mug cake.

Top Bants on Shopping.

Look into any self-help budgeting book and they'll tell you to go shopping when you're not hungry so you don't overspend. Obviously it's a great idea but not always so practical.

Our biggest piece of advice is to work out your approximate weekly budget and then take this cash out of the bank to go to the supermarket. Better still, if your weekly budget is £30, take out just £20. We guarantee you (at the time of going to press) you won't need more.

NOTE: This assumes you do not need to buy for specific dietary needs such as vegetarian, vegan, lactose or gluten intolerant. For people with specific diets... don't panic, we can still do it, though that's in our next book. In the meantime, we encourage you to get inspired and visit our Facebook group, don't forget to share your student veggie and vegan recipes with us too.

We have compiled this brilliant shopping list for you and left space for you to add your own items if you want!

TOP BANTS TOP TIP

When shopping both monthly and weekly look out for those offers that will save you money, 'two for the price of one', look in the reduced section for stuff to use immediately or to freeze etc. when sizing up prices look not just at the prices but at the weights (some brands will have the same sized box but less inside or will change the weights but not the packaging).

Also, one to remember is that, ingredients such as meat and veg is generally cheaper if it is a frozen brand (this may not be the case for ready prepared foods and ready meals though)

Monthly

- 1 packet butter or spreadable butter
- 1 jar of jam / marmalade / peanut butter
- 1 large packet of pasta
- 1 large bag of rice (don't get cook in the bag it's really expensive)
- 8 tins of chopped tomatoes
- 4 tins of tuna
- 1 bottle of oil
- 1 packet of stock cubes (chicken or vegetable)
- 1 box corn flour
- 1 box suet (meat or vegetarian)
- 1 tube of tomato puree
- 1 pot mayonnaise
- Packet of four toilet rolls. We recommend you keep these hidden in your bedroom, as there's always that one toilet roll eater who uses them up!
- 1 jar of lazy garlic, or 1 tube of puree garlic

Weekly

- 2 loaves of bread

TOP BANTS TOP TIP

Look in the discount isle. Freeze both loaves of bread, and take out slices when you need them. You can toast from frozen, and it takes 30 minutes to defrost a normal slice of bread! Buy brown (parents will be impressed). If you don't freeze it then keep it sealed and in the fridge, it will last longer and with less waste.

- 6 eggs. There are so many super quick and tasty things you can make with eggs, easy to boil for egg sandwiches, omelets (especially the Top Bants way), scrambled eggs, pancakes, quiche, the list is endless.
- 4 tins of beans. Get cheap ones! 98p for four vs. £3.85 for the top brand ones. Imagine you use four tins a week. That's £52.92 for the cheap brand, vs. £200.20 saving £147.28 (over the year this equates to 14 bottles of own brand vodka... NOW we have your attention!)
- 1 pint of milk. OK so milk is a funny one, because it goes off. Some authorities recommend it's good for a week beyond its sell by date. Always reach to the back of the display cabinet to get the freshest carton, you can find and check that sell by date. Always keep milk in the fridge, you may find that half way through the week you need more (especially if you eat lots of cereal or are cooking with it) but at around 50p, it's worth buying it in when you need it and not just because you're doing your weekly shop and you used two pints last week!
- 1 packet of cheap cheese. Cheese is great cut up fine in sandwiches with a little salad, popped on top of your jacket potato, shoved in an omelet, and sprinkled over your fave pasta dish. It keeps well in the fridge (keep it well wrapped up) and if you have hard bits on the edge just cut them off and use in a sauce. We don't recommend you use cheese that has gone moldy. Don't buy pre grated cheese, it's really expensive, and far cheaper to cut it small, or buy a grater and do it yourself.

- 2 onions. You can't go wrong with onions. In our other book "Top Bants in the Kitchen" we show you how to cut one without crying heaps. Don't be put off by the crying thing, onions are really versatile and make food taste great! Onions take a while to go off. Typically if kept in the fridge they'll last for a good few weeks!

- Frozen veg. We're recommending this because it's a cheap way to buy and use vegetables without worrying about them going off! You can get all sorts of types of frozen veg, we're recommending you start off with the mixed frozen veg, as it costs less than £1, and it's a good easy introduction to getting some quick health in your diet! It's also really impressive when the parents come to visit, and discover you're attempting to eat healthily, regardless or not of if the packet has even been opened!

TOP BANTS TOP TIP

ALWAYS read freezing instructions on any packet of frozen food, and adhere to these. It's not complicated at all, but can be dangerous if you do not use your freezer correctly.

Frozen veg only stays good if you keep it in the freezer. Alternatively, you can buy a couple of cans of tinned mixed veg for around 40p each!

- Bacon offcuts. Now if you're veggie, just avoid getting these! If you're someone who loves their meat then bacon offcuts are a great way to go. You can also divide the packet up and freeze portions. When buying bacon, always look at the "price per kilo" and not the price of the packet. This is a great rule of thumb when buying most meat products, it will save you a fortune and, if kept in the freezer, will last you a good long time. If you don't have a freezer, check the use by date, keep well wrapped up, and you should be good to keep the packet for a good while but, don't exceed the 'use by date'.

- 1 tin of lentils. Now, if you really want to cut costs we suggest you buy dried lentils but, we have to be real here. You can get a LOT of dried lentils for your money, they're a faff to cook and we guarantee you'll still have them in your cupboard in a years time, so essentially, that's false economy. What we recommend is to buy tins of precooked lentils; they're not expensive and can be turned into the most amazing pasta and curry dishes.

TOP BANTS TOP TIP

Lentils are really healthy and good for you. Take a photo; your parents will be impressed. However, a note of caution, they can cause really bad wind - you have been warned!

- 2 tins of tuna. Tuna is really versatile, if in an unopened tin it will last for a good year, once you've opened the tin though, keep the tuna in a covered bowl in the fridge and it will be good for a few days. You can use tuna for sandwiches, in omelets, in pasta dishes, pie dishes, turn it into a curry, pop it on top of a pizza... oh we're going to discover so many awesome things you can do with a humble can of tuna!

- Frozen peas - top tip, if you don't like them, you can at least use them as a cold compress to put on injuries of housemates that have a fall / bump their head or sprain a wrist. You can also hide them in a huge amount of dishes to get your health quota! They take very little cooking. Please note if you don't have a freezer to store them in, we recommend you buy tinned peas.

- Fresh fruit. Always a good idea for when you're "on the go" and a great way of getting healthy fast food into you. When buying fruit, always compare the price per kilo on prepackaged fruit to loose fruit. If possible, in addition to thinking about your pocket, try to consider plastic wrapping and its effect on the environment.

- Always visit the discounted area, you'll find an abundance of fresh fruit and veg at knock down prices.

Stocking Your Kitchen and Ready to Cook

So, ingredients at the ready you will need some handy kitchen basics that you can't live without, some of this will be included in self-catered halls or with the house contents but some won't. Ask family too for some of these things, often people double up on things that they can pass your way.

- 1 toaster
- 1 large frying pan or wok (or both if you can run to it)
- 1 wooden spatula, 1 wooden spoon
- 1 small saucepan with lid (2 would be awesome)
- 1 sieve or colander
- 1 serving spoon
- 1 x potato masher
- 1 mixing bowl
- 2 dinner plates, side plates, and cereal bowls
- 2 knives, forks and spoons
- 2 soup / cereal bowls
- 2 mugs
- 2 glasses
- 2 sets of chopsticks
- A roll of tin foil
- A large roll of kitchen roll
- Freezer bags (only for students who have access to a freezer)

Not essentials but really useful and money saving;

- A slow cooker - covered in 'Top Bants in the Kitchen'
- A hand blender/mixer
- A microwave oven

Chapter 4

Top Bants on Cooking

Based on the list of ingredients outlined in the previous chapter you are ready for some cooking. First off you need to have a bit of explanation of cooking jargon up front.

Cooking Jargon

Following a Recipe

Recipe books, you'll learn over time, act as a bit of a guide on how to cook something; it's a really really rare occasion when you have to follow the recipe to the letter! But they do look daunting sometimes and send us into a panic and racing to the freezer for that elusive cheap pizza you bought for emergencies.

All our recipes are tried and tested on the most challenged of first year students. We find if you scrub out the complicated words and replace with simple ones, in the first instance, it makes the recipe so much easier.

The following is a simple guide to help you work through the jargon of cooking.

Al dente - this most often applies to pasta. If you see a recipe that says al dente it means just undercook it ever so slightly so that when you bite into it it's slightly firm between your teeth.

Does it make any difference to the end result? No, not if you're a student! It will still taste just as good as if you forget it for a few more minutes and over cook it.

Ignore the words "al dente" and cook it the way you like it, trial and error will work here.

Bake - this means shove it in the oven. Like "bake a cake"

Baste - you've probably heard many stories about turkey basters and semen. If you haven't then just Google it and it will put you off of eating anything that has been basted for your entire life. Basically it means, get some of the juice from the bottom of the pan and tip it on top of the food. Does it make much difference in your student life? It can ensure meat doesn't dry out but frankly, don't waste life worrying about basting!

TOP BANTS TOP TIP

If you are worried about things drying out in the oven either cook in an oven proof container with a lid on or alternatively cover with tin foil.

Batter - This is the crispy stuff on the outside of fish from a fish and chip shop. In Scotland they put batter around Mars Bars and deep fat fry them. Do you need to know about making and using batter? Frankly, it's not a life changer. We'll cover this in a more advanced Top Bants book.

Beat - if you're going to be really pedantic about your cooking you need to know that if you beat something (like a cake mix) you do it to combine all the ingredients really well together. Some people have machines that beat mixes. Honestly though, get a fork and stir it around until the ingredients are well mixed - that's it. If the recipe talks about beating air into the ingredients then this is more complicated but, you can just beat fast and furious until your arm drops off.

Braise - You're hardly going to come across this at the moment but, for the more adventurous of you, if you're cooking a piece of meat you cook it lightly in seasoned butter or oil for a few minutes and then add a little water or stock to cook the meat. It's not a life changer but it's supposed to hold in the flavour of the meat you're cooking!

Cube - this just means cut into squares, the shape and size slightly larger than a dice i.e. just cut it into smallish pieces!

Dice - as above, but into slightly smaller pieces!

Curdle - AVOID all recipes that mention a thread of curdling. Life is too short!

Dollop - you'll rarely see this word in a recipe book but we had to include it as it's just such a great word - DOLLOP! You could have a dollop of mashed potato or a dollop of cream. Unless specified in the recipe a dollop is an un-quantified amount of said food on a spoon that you chuck onto your plate or add to a pan.

Drizzle - this is when you pour a liquid, such as melted chocolate or butter, from a jug or on a spoon in a fine line going backwards and forwards to make it look posh. Alternatively, just dollop as much on as you like and save yourself the pain!

Grate - graters are a really handy piece of kit to add to your kitchen. But let's be real. If you're on a budget and can't afford a grater just chop the stuff into super small bits and you'll be good to go!

A grater from a low cost supermarket at the time of going to print is £2, so it's not going to break the bank!

Grill - most ovens in self-catered halls and student accommodation have a grill built into the oven. You can grill heaps of stuff, cheese on toast, bacon, sausages, bread (to make toast if you don't have a toaster) the list is pretty much endless. The downside to using a grill is that it's lots of extra washing up (we recommend covering the base with tin foil to save yourself some time) and also, you have to keep a close eye on grills because you can very quickly burn your dinner if you're not keeping an eye on it. The upside is the fat from the food you're grilling drops down into the pan below, so the food you're cooking is likely to be less fatty. Have a play with the grill on a Saturday morning when you have time on your hands to see how it works!

Grind - NOT what you think and no relation to the app! We're in the kitchen remember! You may have to grind coffee beans (or you can buy instant or pre ground coffee). You could have to grind spices or simply buy packet pre-ground stuff in the supermarket. Don't waste your life worrying about it! Just be careful not to buy stuff that needs to be ground.

Marinate - this usually applies to meat or fish. Mainly bbq type recipes. It means to soak the meat in a flavoured mix or sauce like, chicken in garlic and lemon. The sauce, being called a marinade. (It's unnecessarily complicated hey) You're usually required to marinate for several hours or overnight. Does it make a big difference to the final outcome? Well yes but, it will still taste good if you don't bother!

Puree - To puree something is to mash it up (preferably to a thick sauce type consistency). You frankly don't need super posh kitchen equipment for all of this, just a simple potato masher will do. Pop into your local pound shop to pick one up. If not a fork will work.

Sauté - means frying something in hot oil. Get a wooden spoon and stir, keep stirring, until the contents turn a slight brown colour (but not black)

Simmer - If you're asked in the recipe to simmer something, this means cook it in liquid just below boiling point… don't panic, you don't need a thermometer! Cook at a temperature where you see small bubbles but they don't burst on the surface. If they start to get bigger and come up to burst, just turn the temperature down a bit.

Stir fry - Stir frying food is the way to go as a student and, we really need to cover this in more depth, so we'll do this in the next chapter! It's quick, easy, you can stir fry pretty much everything, and mix heaps of new and different delicious ingredients together. It's also easy to clean up too! Win win. See next chapter for more details!

Whip - We're not talking 50 shades of whip here! Stay calm if you see a recipe that asks you to whip something. Frankly, at this stage, unless you've had previous experience of baking cakes and you have a recipe that asks you to whip you're entering uncharted territory. Whipping something mainly means beating air into it (see beating above) but lift your hand out of the bowl more to try to get air into the dish.

Ready to Cook?

We're going to spend our first week making some really simple recipes, which will take little preparation, impress your friends and family AND give you a pretty healthy diet. All our recipes here take into consideration cost and time!

Before cooking, always make sure your hands are clean! The utensils you're going to use are clean, and there is enough clear area for you to cook!

Day 1

Breakfast	Fried egg on toast (don't worry, we're going to teach you how to do this)
Lunch	Coronation tuna sandwich
Dinner	Jacket potato with cheesy beans.

Fried Egg on Toast

You will need the following.

A non-stick frying pan (or a wok), a wooden flat spatula (Never use metal cooking utensils with a non-stick frying pan), a toaster, or grill to toast bread.

TOP BANTS TOP TIP

If you don't have access to a toaster, don't despair, fried egg sandwiches are just as delicious!

Ingredients

Oil,
1 egg,
1 - 2 slices of bread,
Butter (for your bread)
Ketchup (if you like)
Salt and pepper (optional)

Preparation

Get your frying pan. If it's new, clean and dry it. It's really important not to use wet frying pans, especially when you're going to heat up oil.

In advance, make your toast in the toaster or get your bread ready on a plate and butter it if you like.

Have you ever cracked an egg open to cook it? If you have, go to next step.
If you haven't, don't panic it's really easy. To start with get a glass or mug and gently bash the egg on the side of the glass until you can see a crack in it.

Using your thumbs, pull the egg apart over the top of the glass and let the insides fall into the glass. It can take a bit of practice so we always recommend you crack the egg over the glass in the first place (and not directly into the pan). If you have shell in the glass stick your fingers in and fish it out!

Put one spoon of oil into the frying pan put it on the hob and turn it on to a medium to high heat.

When cooking with oil, don't leave the room as oil catches fire really easily if unattended as it heats up really quickly. Watch over the oil until you think it's hot. If you're using a gas hob, this is usually quicker than an electric hob.

Place your hand over the top of the frying pan (about 50 cms above the pan), but DO NOT touch it. If you feel heat coming up from the pan then it's time to pop the egg in.

Tip the egg (that you have previously cracked into a glass) gently into the frying pan. Do this gently, because oil can splash up and hot oil hurts!

You will see that slowly the outside of the egg will turn white. Wait until all the clear part of the egg has turned white, if the oil is sizzling and getting a bit hot you may like to turn the temperature down at this point. If you like your yolk runny once the entire outside of the egg has turned white then it's time to take it out of the pan. If you like your yolk hard, grab your spatula, gently slide it underneath the egg and turn the egg over.

Do NOT attempt to toss the egg in the same way as you would a pancake. It's super dangerous, you can get splattered with hot oil and potentially catch light to the pan or the hob. Cook gently on the other side for a minute. Turn the hob off. Slide the egg on to your pre-prepared toast or buttered bread and, bingo, you have fried egg on toast!

You can season your egg now, with a pinch of salt and pepper or just tip ketchup over the top!

TOP BANTS TOP TIP

How to know if your egg is fresh. If your eggs have been sitting around the house for several weeks, you may be worried that they're not good enough to eat.

Eggs last for a surprisingly long time, often months! So before you chuck that egg away, check to see if it's fresh. Get a jug of cold water or fill up a mug with water. Put the whole egg, (in its shell) gently into the jug or mug. If the egg floats then it's most definitely off, so chuck it away! If the egg sinks then it's absolutely fine to use!

TOP BANTS TOP TIP

Three useful tips when using oil!

1. Don't put hot frying pans into cold bowls of water. Leave them to cool down on the hob. Only put water on once they have cooled down.

2. Oil burns, and an oil burn can be really bad. If you get hot oil on your hands, arms or skin, run a cold tap over the affected area for a good 10 minutes. If the pain continues, or the affected area is large, speak to your local pharmacist or doctor immediately.

3. If the pan accidentally catches on fire <u>never ever ever throw water</u> on it, turn off the heat source and if it continues to burn get a cloth, wet it under the tap, but not enough to drip water, just enough to make it moist, and completely cover the pan with it to extinguish the flames.

    Remember that old fire and oxygen tip from Chemistry?

Coronation Tuna Sandwich

You will need a plate, a sharp knife, a small mixing bowl, a teaspoon.

Ingredients

½ tin of tuna
½ an onion chopped small (optional)
Mayonnaise
½ teaspoon of curry powder
1 teaspoon of ketchup
2 dessert spoons of sweet corn, (optional)
1 Fresh tomato (optional)
Some lettuce (optional).

Preparation

Open your tin of tuna. With the lid still on the top of the tuna, tip away the juice from within the tin, you can tip this down the drain, but be careful to keep the lid in place or the tuna will fly out all over the place! You only want to use ½ the tin for this sandwich. Take the other half, and put in a covered bowl in the fridge (you will use this later in the week).
Tip the tuna you need into a bowl.
Add ½ a teaspoon of curry powder to the tuna and stir in well.
Add 2 - 4 soup spoons of mayonnaise, and stir.
Add the optional onion, sweet corn, and tomato if you like.
Add a blob of ketchup to the mix (optional)

Make your sandwich super healthy by using up any items you may have in the fridge, this includes any leftover vegetables chopped up small, a few lettuce leaves, some chopped up fresh tomato.

Get another piece of buttered bread and pop it over the top, and voila… you have a super cool coronation tuna sandwich!

TOP BANTS TOP TIP

You can swap tuna for bits of cooked diced chicken, sliced boiled egg, cooked bacon bits, or any other precooked meat. You could even replace the tuna with diced cheese!

Vegan option - replace tuna with cooked butter beans, and butter with a vegan spread, replace mayonnaise with vegan mayonnaise.

Jacket Potato with Beans and Cheese

You will need a plate, a fork, a pan, tin opener, grater and a knife

Ingredients

1 or 2 potatoes
Some cheese
Baked beans
Some oil
Salt and pepper
Preparation

Get a good sized potato or two. Wash under the tap, using a fork stab the potato about 5 - 6 times around the outside (this stops the potato exploding).

Pour a little oil (about a teaspoon full) on to your hand, add a pinch of salt and pepper.

With your hands, rub the outside of the potato until it has a little oil all around the outside.
Put the potato onto a microwave proof plate.

Pop the microwave setting on to "high" and cook for 7 minutes. Open up the microwave, and stab the potato with a fork, at the top and the bottom. (Be careful not to touch the potato, it will be HOT)

If the fork goes in easily the potato is cooked. If not, turn the potato over and cook on high for an extra two to three minutes.

Leave the potato to cool down on the side for 5 minutes before serving with your choice of topping.

Jacket Potato in the Oven

Turn on the oven to Gas Mark 6, 180 - 200 C

Jacket potatoes in our opinion are far better if cooked in the oven, they have that lovely crispy crunchy skin that reminds you of home and are delicious. The big problem is though that they take a lot longer to cook. So you have to manage your time a bit better. Essentially, it takes no more of your preparation time but, you do need to consider baking them about an hour before you want them!

TOP BANTS TOP TIP

If you microwave the potato for 3 or 4 minutes before putting it in the oven you will have the best of both worlds, speed and extra yumminess.

Follow the same steps as with a microwave jacket potato (as above)

Pop the prepared potato onto a tray in the oven, or on a bit of tin foil on the rack (do not wrap the potato in the tin foil unless you like it soggy)

Put into the oven for about an hour!

Now for the all-important topping.

Bean topping. Open a can of baked beans, heat beans up in microwave, or in a saucepan on the hob.

Stir occasionally until you can see bubbles coming up around the edge; make sure to stir the middle of the pan too, so that the beans don't stick.

When you think they're hot enough - usually about 3 - 5 minutes. Take the pan off of the hob, and turn the hob off. Cut a cross into the top of the jacket potato to open it up a bit and pour beans over the top.

Optional

- Pop grated or finely chopped cheese on top.
- Add ½ a teaspoon of curry powder to the beans to make them spicy.
- Throw in some precooked vegetables with the beans and heat up.
- Separately fry some onions and bacon and sprinkle over the top.

Day 2

Breakfast	Toast
Lunch	BLT sandwich
Dinner	Beans and Pasta

Something on Toast

We already know how to fry an egg - see day one again if you've forgotten. But there's nothing better than something yummy on toast. In your cupboard you should have your bread, butter and topping. Grab your favourite and get making heaps of toast with it.

TOP BANTS TOP TIP

Keep jam and marmalade in the fridge, and always use a clean knife when you're getting some out of the jar, this will prevent it from going off so quickly! Marmite and peanut butter can be kept in a normal cupboard!

BLT sandwich with or without the B, the L or the T

Ingredients

Bacon, lettuce, tomato.
Slices of bread
Butter or mayonnaise
For an optional 'O' add some onion.

Preparation

BLT sandwiches are simply delicious and easy to prepare. Don't be put off by the fact that you've got to cook the bacon, it's easy!

Spread your bread with butter or mayonnaise.

If you're a first time bacon chef then there are several ways you can do it!

Cook bacon in the oven, fry, grill or microwave it.

For now, we're going to keep things as simple, fast and least messy as possible! (After all, we want to minimise our washing up pile). So we're going to microwave our bacon.

Grab some kitchen roll. Put two squares of kitchen roll onto a plate. Get three pieces of bacon, or enough to cover your bread, (remember bacon shrinks, so you'll want the equivalent of 2 - 3 rashers if you're using bacon pieces).

Pop the bacon onto the kitchen roll, then cover with another two pieces of kitchen roll. Pop in to the microwave for 3 - 5 minutes. Take the kitchen roll off of the top and bottom of the bacon, and leave bacon to cool.

Lay your cooked bacon slices onto the bread. So you have the 'B' then chuck the 'L' and the 'T' on top. BLT's are also great cold. Cook up extra bacon, then leave it to cool before you make the sandwich.

The sandwich will keep well for the day, and is great to eat in lectures!

TOP BANTS TOP TIP

Turn your BLT into a toasted BLT for a bit of a change by toasting your bread first! This is also a great way of using up old bread that has gone a bit dry!

Beans and pasta "Basta"

Ingredients

1 tin of baked beans,
1 tin of tomatoes, or tin of condensed tomato soup
½ an onion, (optional)
1 tea spoon full of mixed herbs,
1 spoon of lazy garlic or garlic puree,
2 large spoons of ketchup,
½ cup mixed frozen vegetables, or a small tin of mixed vegetables.
Cheese as much as you want (finely cut or grated)
Bacon (optional)

Preparation

If using an onion cut your onion up and pop it into a frying pan with a small spoon of oil, turn on the heat to a medium setting and cook the chopped onions until they start to go brown. Add some lazy garlic or garlic puree and ½ a spoon of mixed herbs. Stir around for 1-2 minutes and take off of the heat.

Pop the frozen vegetables into a non-metallic bowl. Add ¼ cup of water cover the bowl and cook in the microwave on full for 3 minutes. When cooked drain the water out.

Pop the fried onion and seasoning mix into a bowl or pan with the cooked vegetables, open the tin of beans and the tin of tomatoes, and add these to the bowl or pan.
Add ketchup and salt and pepper.
Stir it all together.
Split this mixture in half (you're going to use half tomorrow so pop it in the fridge)

If using bacon, now is the time to cook it in the microwave (see BLT recipe). Once cooked set the bacon aside to use later.

Fill a small saucepan half full with water. Put a pinch of salt into the water.

When the water is boiling, add 2 mugs of dried pasta. Look at the instructions on the packet for the amount of time you need to cook the pasta. Every make cooks at a different speed.

Make sure that your saucepan of water does not boil over. If it looks like its boiling too much and bubbling over the top take it off of the heat and turn the heat down.

Once the pasta has cooked (as per the instructions on the packet) take it off of the hob,

Catch a bit of pasta with a fork and have a taste to see if it is cooked to your preference.

Holding the sieve in one hand, tip the pasta and water through the sieve, catching the pasta in the sieve and shake it gently to get all the water out.

Mix the pasta with the sauce, and pop in the microwave on full power for two minutes.

Open the microwave door, and stir the mixture with a spoon. Put back in the microwave on full power for an extra two minutes.

Take the bowl out and leave the mixture to cool for one minute. Tip it onto a plate and serve with your optional bacon bits or some grated cheese if you like!

Day 3

Breakfast   Last night's leftovers
Lunch   Omelet
Dinner   Mixed bean curry

Breakfast Leftovers

The cool thing about being a student is that you ARE allowed to eat last night's leftovers for breakfast! Leftovers come in many forms, old kebabs, old chips (though we think they're pretty lame), scraggy bits of pizza… the list is endless, and so we really recommend either just heating up some of last night's dinner in the microwave, and pouring it over a piece of toast, or easier still, chucking it in a sandwich! The choice is yours!

Omelet

Ingredients

A spoon of oil for the pan
2-4 Eggs, cheese, seasoning like salt and pepper.

Preparation

OK so don't panic here, omelets aren't actually so hard to make but, there is a knack to them! We may call our first omelet scrambled egg but, that's fine too (unless of course you don't like scrambled eggs or indeed eggs, in which case, you'll have to have toast for breakfast, and last nights left overs for lunch). Omelets are a great way of using up old stuff in the fridge, this could be some cheese, an old onion, bits of bacon, or tuna, or even some vegetables.

As we're trying to keep things easy this week we're just going to make a cheese omelet!

You will need that non-stick frying pan - let's hope you have washed it up since you used it, if not do it now and let it dry. Same goes for that wooden spatula we used it to make that fried egg two days ago, if it's not washed… again, now is the time to do this!

First grate your cheese, or chop it into little bits if you don't have a grater!

Next crack your eggs into a bowl or a jug, or a very large mug, take out all the bits of shell that may have fallen into the mug with the egg.

Add a pinch of salt and pepper if you fancy and, with a fork mix the eggs together.

Get your frying pan and put in a spoon full of oil. Pop it on the hob, on a medium heat in the same way you would with a fried egg!

When the oil in the pan is hot enough tip your egg mixture into the frying pan and quickly stir around until the egg starts to cook and form lumps. This is when you stop stirring it.

The egg at the bottom will be cooking but you will see the egg on the top will still be runny. Turn the temperature down so that you don't burn the bottom!

Leave this to cook for another minute, until the egg on the top is less runny.

Get your spatula and push the sides of the omelet in the pan, when you see the egg coming away from the edge, you know it's starting to cook well.

Look out for our Insta video under #dontbelikestephen #topbants #omelet

Tip the bits of cheese onto the top of the omelet.

As the top of the omelet starts to solidify, grab your spatula and slide it underneath one half of the omelet to fold it over into a semicircle.

Leave to cook for another minute on a low heat, and then leave for a further minute for the egg in the middle to solidify

TOP BANTS TOP TIP

Get a plate that is larger than the size of your frying pan. Pop the plate over the frying pan when you're ready to serve. Holding the plate in place with your left hand, pick up the pan with your right hand, and turn them over so that the plate is underneath the frying pan.

The omelet should just drop onto the plate in one piece! (Do this the opposite way if you're left handed.)

Keep this dish cheap by serving with some toast and even make it healthy by serving it with tomatoes and salad.

Stick your head in the fridge to see if you can find some left over vegetables or use a spoonful of last night's bean dish to jazz it up a bit!

Mixed Bean Curry

Ingredients

Your leftover bean mix from last night
2 teaspoons of curry powder
1 large spoon of oil
1 cup of rice

Preparation

Remember that bean mix we saved last night? Right, this evening we're going to cook it up and turn it into a curry!

Get that frying pan from lunch, it doesn't matter if you didn't wash it up. Just get a piece of kitchen roll and wipe it around the pan to get the omelet remains off!

Put the hob onto a medium heat.

Get a spoon full of oil, and put it into the pan. Grab your packet of curry powder, and pop 1 - 2 teaspoons of the powder into the oil.

Stir it around gently until it starts to get a bit thick and the powder has become a paste with the oil, don't let the oil get too hot or the mix will go black and be disgusting.
Keep stirring for 1 - 2 minutes on a low heat.

Let the mixture cool for a bit, and then tip it into the bean mix and stir it in thoroughly.

Heat the bean mix in the microwave for 2 - 3 minutes, and then leave it there, whilst you concentrate on the rice.

Now we're going to cook rice!

Grab that saucepan and make sure it's clean! Half fill it with water and add a pinch of salt. Turn the hob on a high heat and pop the pan with the water onto the hob and bring it to the boil.

In the meantime grab your packet of rice. Most people suggest that you need half a cup of dried rice per person, we've suggested one cup, because it still comes within our budget and, worst case you can invite a friend to join you!

So measure out 1 cup of rice and put this in a bowl!

TOP BANTS TOP TIP

We always recommend getting packets of loose rice, and not boil in a bag rice. Rice is easy enough to cook and it costs far less if you cook this from scratch!

Wash your rice, sounds strange but put the rice into a bowl and fill the bowl with water, swish it around the bowl with your hands for 30 seconds to wash the starch off!

Get your sieve and tip the rice and water through the sieve, tip the rice back in the bowl add more clean water and swish around again. Repeat this for another two or three times until the water runs clear. It's not the end of the world if you don't do this, but if you don't you'll need to rinse the rice extra well at the end to stop it going gloopy!

If you're cooking rice for the first few times just accept it's always a bit hit and miss as each rice brand is different and sometimes cooking it can take a bit of practice!

Stick to the instructions on the packet in terms of cooking time!

Always add rice to boiling water and not to cold water, as this will affect your cooking time and quality of your end dish!

Having followed the instructions on the packet we are now assuming you have your rice ready and cooked.

Once cooked, pour the rice into your sieve or colander, and pour over a kettle of boiling water to give the rice one last clean!

TOP BANTS TOP TIP

Add a small knob of butter (about a teaspoonful) to the rice once you have drained it, and stir it around. This stops it sticking.

Turn your microwave on to full with the bean mix in and cook for a further 2 minutes.

In the meantime, tip your rice onto a plate.

Get the bean curry mix out of the microwave and serve with the rice, yummy.

Day 4

Breakfast
Just about anything goes on toast! Start experimenting!

Lunch
Cheese sandwiches! Crisp sandwiches, got some salad left?
Chuck this in too…

TOP BANTS sandwiches have literally ANYTHING in them!
Even left over curry from last night!

Dinner
Fried rice! YUM!
Here goes to a super quick and really delicious fried rice
recipe.

Egg fried rice - the simple version

Ingredients

1 cup cooked rice
A knob of butter
2 eggs opened up and put in a cup without shell bits,
A few bits of bacon,
½ an onion,
1 vegetable or chicken stock cube
A handful of frozen peas, or sweet corn. (or peas/sweet corn
from a tin).
1 spoon of oil

Preparation

Cook up one cup of rice, once cooked, drain the rice and stir in the knob of butter.

Grab a chicken or vegetable stock cube, crumble it into a really fine powder between your fingers and mix into the rice along with the knob of butter and frozen or tinned sweet corn or peas or both.

Put a spoon full of oil into your pan.

Cut up ½ an onion and cut the bacon you have into small pieces (about the same size as the onion you have cut).

Put the pan (or wok) onto the hob and turn on to heat the oil - in the same way we did when we were frying the egg!

Chuck the bacon and onion into the pan and cook until the onion starts to go brown. Tip the contents onto a plate.

Pop the pan back on to the heat and chuck in the egg, mix it around until it's the same consistency as scrambled egg.

Pop everything back into the pan. Lower the heat, and stir around for 5 minutes to cook everything through.

Tip onto a plate and add salt and pepper to taste! Bang!

Day 5

Breakfast	Toast or a fried egg sandwich
Lunch	Pizza Top Bants style!
Dinner	Tuna bake with a cheese sauce

Breakfast

Toast, or perhaps a fried egg, or perhaps fried egg on toast, or a fried egg sandwich... even with a bit of microwaved bacon in it! Let's face it - you're already able to cook quite a bit, and that's just after four days!

Top Bants Pizza

Ingredients

Sliced bread,
A dollop of ketchup,
Grated or sliced cheese,
½ and onion, (optional)
Garlic (optional)
1 spoon of oil
A slice or two of cooked bacon,
A good squirt of tomato puree, if you don't have it, leave it out
1 teaspoon of mixed herbs
Half a tomato

Preparation

We all love a pizza, but just HOW expensive are they! Today's lunch is a Top Bants Pizza, quite possibly the cheapest and easiest pizza life can bring you as a student!

You can be really gross with this, and make it the "lads way" or slightly more sophisticated, and make a top notch attempt… let's look at the lads pizza first.

Make some toast
Put some ketchup on the toast
Cut up a bit of cheese (just a few slices)
Pop the toast under the grill for a few minutes until the cheese has melted.

Voila… Top Bants lads pizza!

For a more sophisticated edge to your pizza you will need the list of ingredients above!

So first of all, toast a couple of pieces of bread!

Chop up your onions and bacon. Mix together.

Put a spoon full of oil in the frying pan, turn on the hob to a medium heat and, as with the fried egg, when it becomes hot add the onions and bacon and fry up until the onions start to turn brown.

Add the lazy garlic or puree, 2 spoons of tomato puree, mixed herbs and stir the mixture until it all becomes hot.

Tip the mixture onto your pieces of toast and spread evenly all over with a knife.

Pop your thin slices of tomato onto the toast and then the grated cheese.

Pop under the grill for a few minutes until the cheese has melted and bingo… Top Bants pizza!

Tuna bake with cheese sauce

Ingredients

½ tub of creme fraiche,
½ onion,
½ tin of tuna,
½ cup of frozen peas or sweet corn, or both, or a can of mixed vegetables,
2 cups of dried pasta.
½ cup cheese, grated or cut into small pieces.

Preparation

First cook your pasta. Remember to follow the rules on the packet, put the pasta into boiling water to cook, and don't forget about it.

Once the pasta is cooked, empty the hot water out of the saucepan and fill the pan with the pasta in it with cold water as this will stop it sticking together for now.

Leave the pasta on the side to cool down.

Next chop your onion and cook it in a frying pan with a spoon full of oil, keep stirring until the onion starts to go brown.

Add, ½ a tub of creme fraiche, ½ tin of tuna, the frozen peas / sweet corn or both and any pre-cooked vegetables you have lying around to the pan.

Slowly stir the mixture on a low heat until the cream is hot.

Add pasta to the creamy mixture in the pan and heat for another two minutes at a medium heat.

Take off the heat and stir in the grated cheese. Serve ⅔ of the mixture on a plate. (Keep the rest for lunch tomorrow in the fridge) it's nice cold too! You can make it look really funky by adding a few basil leaves onto the top!

Garlic bread is a classy addition to this creation of yumminess. See the following chapter for how to make this.

Day 6

Breakfast - Cheese on toast / omelet / toast with ANYTHING!
Lunch - Last night's pasta dish
Dinner - Easy lentil curry / or curry with your advanced cooking skills

Breakfast - Cheese on toast.

You need

Some cheese, you can slice it or grate it. (It tends to go a bit further if it's grated)
Sliced bread that you have toasted in the toaster.

Pop the cheese onto the sliced bread. Pop it under the grill and keep an eye on it. Depending on the strength of your grill, it should be nicely melted within a few minutes, and just a minute or two later, should start going brown. Take it out when it's cooked to your preference, and serve.
Spice it up a bit by tipping a bit of Worcester sauce or Tabasco sauce over it during the cooking process!

TOP BANTS TOP TIP

You could make this healthy and pop some thinly sliced tomatoes on top or underneath the cheese.

Lunch - last night's pasta, served hot or cold - it'll be delicious! If you're at home, you could cook up some vegetables to go with it, or in it!

If you're in lectures, take it with you in a container and enjoy it cold!

Stephen from our team didn't have a container. He decided to recycle and pop his pasta in an old crisp packet. We love recycling, but really... a crisp packet? #dontbelikestephen.

Easy lentil curry – serves two people.

3 desert spoons of oil
½ onion, chopped
1 - 2 teaspoons lazy garlic or garlic puree
2 - 3 teaspoons curry powder
1 stock cube (chicken or vegetable)
1 tin cooked lentils (opened)
1 tin tomatoes (opened)
½ cup of water
1 tin precooked vegetables or 1 cup frozen vegetables (optional)

Pop the oil in the pan, heat up and add the onions. Cook until the onions are brown. Add the curry powder and stir until it forms a paste. Add the garlic, cook for another minute or two on a slightly cooler heat and then take off the heat and stir.

Chuck the opened tinned lentils and tomatoes in a saucepan. Add the stock cube, and onion curry paste that you have just made, add the water and optional vegetables.

Place the saucepan on the hob, and cook (stirring regularly) for 15 minutes. Try not to let it boil, or burn at the bottom of the pan. If you feel it is getting too hot, turn down the heat on the hob.

In the meantime make some rice (we have done this already remember?)

Reheat the curry mixture up and serve with the rice. To be extra healthy, you could serve with salad or some vegetables.

Advanced Curry

It's a really bizarre thing, but most of our parents really don't know how to make a good curry from scratch, and yet it's so easy and so cheap to make it at home... AND it tastes delicious.

For this recipe, we're not just going to teach you how to make just about any basic curry ever, but we're also going to teach you how to make poppadum's from scratch (only because we've just learnt to do it ourselves, they were super easy, and super impressive)

Ingredients

The fun thing about student curries, is that you can use just about anything you like. You just need a few essentials to get you going.

Essentials - for two servings.

1 onion finely chopped (although optional but just about every curry has onions in it)
Garlic / lazy garlic / puree or fresh finely chopped
3 - 5 teaspoons of Curry Powder (we like the Medium Madras, but a stronger or mild powder will do)
If you want to be super cool, mix turmeric, cumin, coriander, ginger, cardamom and chili powder together and use instead of a curry powder.
Oil (a few spoonful's)
Stock cube (vegetable or chicken)

1 litre (or 2 - 3 mugful's of water)
3 teaspoons of corn flour (to thicken the curry at the end)
To make it "fancy" as Phoebe from our team so bluntly puts it.
You can use the following (but they're all optional - chuck
them in if you have them and can afford them, or simply leave
them out if not).

Section 1 - seasoning

1 large spoonful fresh ginger grate or chop finely (find this in
the vegetable aisle)
1 large spoonful of lemon grass - chopped finely (in the fresh
herb section)
½ a Coconut block (in the curry section)
2 teaspoons of chili powder (if you want it extra spicy - also in
the curry section)
1 teaspoon of black cumin seeds (curry section of the
supermarket)
2 large spoonfuls of fresh coriander - (Herb section of the
supermarket. You can chuck some in at the beginning or leave
it to sprinkle on the curry at the end to make it look
awesome).

Section 2 - meat

Cut all meat into cubes, typically just a bit bigger than a dice.
For two servings you need 1 large mug full of diced meat.

Once you have cut the meat up, fry it separately in a frying
pan until it's gone slightly brown (but not black) Once fried,
cook in the saucepan for the following times (see info below)

Chicken or turkey (25 minutes)
Pork (25 minutes)
Lamb (40 minutes)

Beef (40 minutes)
Minced beef (of course you don't need to cut this as it's minced already, just break it apart as you put it in the pan) (20 minutes)
Section 3 - Vegetables

As above, you can use any of the following; you may find them in your fridge or the discounted section of the supermarket.

For two servings you want three large mugs of diced vegetables from the selection below, if you're a veggie, or don't have meat, simply use 4 large mugs of diced vegetables. In the brackets below you can see how long you need to cook them for.

So, when you are dicing vegetables, obviously you don't want to cut up lentils, but you can chop up the tomatoes that are in a tin. It really doesn't matter what shape you cut your vegetables, so long as they are not much bigger than a dice, but just experiment with this!

Red, green or yellow peppers (5 minutes - because we like ours crunchy)
Fresh or tinned tomatoes (5 minutes - because they just need heating through)
Cabbage (5 minutes because we don't like it mushy)
Peas or sweet corn (5 minutes)
Frozen vegetables (5 minutes - because they will cool down the water & need to be served hot)
Tinned vegetables (3 minutes). Just to heat through
Courgette (5 minutes because we like it crunchy)
Tinned lentils (5 minutes)
Cauliflower or fresh carrots (10 minutes)

Potatoes (20 minutes fresh / 5 minutes if precooked from a can)
More onions (chuck in the pan 10 minutes before the end of cooking if you like them crunchy)
More garlic! (Chuck in whenever… but remember, it's not great to stink of garlic)
Just about any other vegetables you can think of
> Root vegetables (10 - 20 minutes)
> Green vegetables (5 - 8 minutes)

Preparation

NOW FOR A BIT OF MAGIC - because it's really so simple!

Pop the oil on to heat in the pan.
Add the onions and garlic cook them well until the onions go slightly brown.
Add the curry powder / spices for the curry, and stir for a further 3 - 5 minutes until you have a paste.
Pop this on a plate to one side.
Add a little more oil to the pan and anything you like from section 2, and cook on a low heat, stir all of the ingredients constantly for 4 – 5 minutes.
Tip all of this into a large saucepan.
Add the water and the stock cube, and pop it on to the hob to simmer.
Add the prepared meat from SECTION 2 (optional) that has been sautéed
Add the prepared vegetables from SECTION 3

Two really important things will start to happen as you're cooking this;

1. The water will evaporate. Just add more water to ensure the top of the mixture is just covered.
2. You will find friends you never knew you had rocking up to get an invite! That's OK, get them to contribute with some food or alcohol, and chuck in some extra vegetables for good measure!

When the curry is just about ready to eat, you'll notice this should still be a bit liquidy (because you'll have been topping it up with water whilst it's been cooking). Don't panic, this is where the corn flour comes in handy. Pop 2 large tea spoons of the corn flour into a mug or glass.

Fill the cup to just above halfway with cold water and stir until you have no lumps. Take the curry off of the heat, and quickly tip the corn flour and water mix into the pan, stirring really quickly. If your curry isn't thick enough, you can add more corn flour as above and heat up the curry one more time stirring constantly. Your curry is now ready to serve.

RICE
It would be great if about 35 minutes before the curry was ready, that you could cook the rice. We're being realistic, if this is your first time cooking a curry, and you may have other things on your mind. So, our suggestion is, that you pop the curry to one side once cooked, and then cook the rice. You can simply reheat the curry.

TOP BANTS TOP POPPADOMS

Poppadom's... OMG! They add that extra special something to a curry, but are always so expensive for us students.

Stephen from the Top Bants team claims he could just live on poppadom's and chips #dontbelikestephen!

None of us knew how easy they were to make, until Hannah piped up with this little gem of a recipe from her grandmother, so here we go - super cheap poppadom's that you can make and eat at any time, even with chips, and even for breakfast! You are… after all, a student!

Poppadoms ingredients

2 cups plain flour
¼ cup water
2 cups oil
Salt and pepper
Cumin seeds (optional)

And then
An extra cup of flour (we'll explain in a bit)
Kitchen roll
A rolling pin (but you can use an empty glass bottle if you don't have one)
You'll also need a frying pan. If you don't have one, ask to borrow one in exchange for a poppadom!

Tip the two cups of flour, water, salt and pepper and cumin seeds if you have them into a bowl. If you don't have cumin seeds just leave them out).

Mix until it's a dough consistency, like the stuff you used to play with as a child!
Sprinkle a good handful of flour onto the place where you're going to roll your poppadom's flat.

Take off a small piece of the dough, and roll into a ball about 2 cm's diameter.

Put the ball on the flour you have sprinkled and roll flat with your rolling pin or glass bottle

After 2 - 3 rolls, turn the poppadom over, and roll the other side.

Keep rolling until the dough is super thin.

Cover with flour each side, and pop onto a piece of kitchen roll.

Cover with another piece of kitchen roll to separate it from the next poppadom.

Continue doing this until you have used up all the dough.

Cooking your Poppadoms;

Put some oil in your frying pan. (Do not fill this more than ¼ full of oil)
Heat up the oil just enough to be hot, (have the dial on the cooker on a medium heat)
Pop in the first rolled poppadom and watch the magic happen.
Leave for a good minute or two until its golden brown on the bottom.
Carefully turn the poppadom over and cook on the other side for about 30 seconds.
(We used a wooden spoon and a fork to turn them over)

DO NOT TOUCH THE POPPADOM… its hot!

Lift the poppadom out of the frying pan and allow the hot oil to drip off, pop on a plate, allow to cool for a short while and eat it!

Do the same with the rest of the dough, using 2 cm pieces. Until you have used up all the dough.

TOP BANTS TOP TIP

Poppadom's will keep for a good few hours (unless of course you just eat them all) so, it's a great idea to make them in advance of a party.

You can always pop them in a warm oven for 5 minutes to warm and crisp up again before serving!

Day 7 - A Sunday Feast!

Brunch   Eggy bread!
Dinner   Last night of the week 'mishmash'

Eggy bread

Ingredients

Sliced bread, eggs, milk or water
This is a great way to use up any old slices of dried bread, just
check it's not gone moldy!
Salt and pepper to taste

Preparation

Nothing like a cooked breakfast to get those brain cells
moving! Eggy bread /Pain perdu, or French toast! Call it what
you like but it's an awesome way to start your day.

TOP BANTS TOP TIP

One is really never enough, so always make at least two
pieces!

You will need 1 egg for every two slices of bread you use and
milk (or water if you have no milk left).

The Top Bants team reckons this is great served with tomato
ketchup!

Crack your egg and pop into a cup (like we did on day one with our fried egg). Check for shell bits! Grab the larger half of your egg shell, and pour milk (or water) into this half, tip this in with the egg. With a fork mix up the egg and milk (or water) and add a pinch of salt and pepper. Once mixed, tip the egg mixture onto a shallow plate.

Grab your frying pan (let's hope it's clean) IF NOT... you know what you need to do! Once it's clean (and dry), put onto the hob onto a medium to high temperature with a spoon full of oil (like we did with the fried egg). Hold your hand over the pan to feel the temperature, but don't put your hand or fingers into the hot oil. Once the oil has got hot...

Grab each piece of bread and dip quickly into the eggy mixture, and cover both sides of the bread. Pop the egg covered bread into the hot oil into the frying pan, and fry gently on both sides until the bread has gone light brown! (It takes just a few minutes) Take each piece out and pop on a plate. Smother with tomato ketchup and BANG... eggy bread!

It's the end of week one! WHOOP WHOOP you've survived! The really cool thing to understand is that in most cases, you don't have to weigh food, you just have to start to understand what types of food go with other types of food, and understand how to cook them, and for how long, it's really not rocket science... it really is TOP BANTS!

So now it's time, to fish everything out of your fridge that's left (check the use by dates), chuck it together and see what happens! It's TOP BANTS mish mash night! DARE you! Don't forget to post to Instagram #topbants, and #dontbelikestephen!

You could air on the side of caution... James from the Top Bants Team has the world's BEST chili recipe (according to him). The cool thing is, it's super easy, and he's adapted it over the last two years depending on his available budget.

James' Famous Chilli - serves 2
The fun thing about chilli is you can chuck just about anything in it, and you have a really great meal! Ok it's not a typical authentic chilli, but as a student anything goes hey, so we've cobbled together this no fail recipe for you to have a play with in your kitchen, as it's the end of the week, we've compiled this to serve two people, as we're guessing you'll be catching up with friends.

Section 1 is your basic ingredients to start off, section 2 is for the meat eaters; section 3 for the vegetarians or those that want vegetables in their chilli.

SECTION 1

½ an onion (finely chopped)
A spoon of lazy garlic / puree / or a clove of fresh garlic (finely chopped)
A stock cube
1 tin of tomatoes
2 - 4 teaspoons of chilli
2 tablespoons of oil
½ litre of water

SECTION 2

Some meat. Just any meat from the fridge or freezer, really finely chopped. Enough to fill one large mug.

SECTION 3

Lots of vegetables finely chopped (smaller than diced) enough to fill 2 - 3 large mugs. Literally use this time to use up all the vegetables from your fridge. Great veg to use are;
Carrots
Squash
Potatoes
Cabbage
Peas / sweet corn you don't need to chop these.
Frozen or canned vegetables (if the pieces are small, you don't need to chop these)
Leeks
Tinned lentils, kidney beans, chick peas
Any ½ opened tins of baked beans. Or just chuck a whole can in if you have it, then you'll have extra prepared food for tomorrow.

How to make your chilli.

Put 2 tablespoons of oil in your pan and cook onions until golden brown. Add the chili powder and stir for a few minutes until the oil absorbs the powder and it becomes a paste, keep stirring. Add the tin of tomatoes, ½ litre of water, garlic and a stock cube.

Bring the ingredients of the pan slowly up to the boil. Chuck in the finely chopped meat, boil for 15 minutes.

Throw in in your selected ingredients from section 3. Cook for 15 minutes. Stir every few minutes. If the mixture gets a bit dry, add a little more water.

Keep stirring the chilli until it's the consistency you like.
EAT!

James likes to serve his chilli with sweet potato, other Top Bants recommendations are to serve with;

Rice, Pasta, Jacket potato, Tacos, Tortillas, Chips, Poppadom's Worst case, a few slices of bread or toast will be just great. Stephen eats his with crisps. #dontbelikestephen.

Chapter 5

Top Bants on Indulgence, Poverty and the Aftermath

Cooking a birthday cake

Someone in your halls or class has a birthday and you want to give them something special that doesn't cost a fortune. It's time to pull out all the stops, and create a special birthday masterpiece, for little or no money! Don't panic, the team at TOP BANTS have it covered!

1. The Mug Cake! Go to a charity shop, and buy the largest mug you can find. We did it just this week, and came home with a really funky looking owl mug that cost us 80p. We're pretty sure if you shop around, you can get a really great one for under £1! It's not about the mug however; it's what you're going to do with it that will make this birthday extra special!

You're going to make the cheapest, easiest most memorable cake your friend has ever had, it's a chocolate mug cake, it WILL taste delicious and it will, most importantly, be cheap and easy!

You can even impress the parents with this great cake when you get home and need your laundry doing for you. So here's how you do it!

Get your mug (make sure it's ok to go in the microwave) typically you're looking for a plain mug, or something that doesn't have any metal bands around it in a silver or gold colour. Give the mug a good wash before you use it!

Ingredients

3 tablespoons of self-raising flour
3 tablespoons of sugar
3 tablespoons of drinking chocolate powder
3 tablespoons of milk
2 tablespoons of vegetable oil (vegetable oil will be fine)

Preparation

Chuck all the ingredients into a bowl and mix really well until there are no lumps or dry bits. Fill your mug to 2/3 with the mixed ingredients. Cook in your microwave on full power for 1 - 2 minutes. (You'll have to experiment with the time you allow, as it will depend on the strength of your microwave).

Leave in the microwave for 2 minutes, make sure it is cool and give to your friend!

You can pop optional bits of chocolate in the mix before you cook it. The Top Bants team like a few slices of Mars bar, or a spoon full of hazelnut spread in there to add to the gooeyness!

For extra effect, try and blag some free candles from the charity shop where you buy the mug or from a friend. We can pretty much guarantee someone has a spare candle!

Stephen from the Top Bants team recalls a story of a time he didn't have candles, so he used a match! #dontbelikestephen!

Cooking for one

Bizarrely it's just as expensive and time consuming cooking for one as it is cooking for two. So you have several choices, always make a bit more and then you have a spare meal for another day or, better still, invite a friend or flat mate to join you to eat. It's more fun eating in a crowd, and also leaves someone else to do the washing up afterwards, and/or to provide the alcohol. It's just a win win situation!

Making food go further

Garlic bread is super cheap and easy to make, and it's less than 40% of the price of pre made garlic bread in the supermarket!

Buy a baguette, lay it out long ways. From left to right… or right to left, slice the bread along the width of the loaf, making sure you don't cut the whole way through, or indeed, cut your fingers!

Get some spreadable butter or margarine. Take out a few dollops, put this in a bowl with some lazy garlic or garlic puree, and a pinch of mixed herbs and mash it together with a fork.

Shove a small dollop of the butter mix between each cut on the baguette. If you have foil, wrap the baguette in foil, but if you don't, then simply pop the baguette in the oven on a low heat, and cook for about 10 – 20 minutes, adding an extra 5 minutes if it's in foil.

If you want to jazz up the recipe, and make it super posh, get a packet of Mozzarella cheese, break it up and pop it between each segment! Or simply cut (or grate) some cheap Cheddar or Emmental cheese and chuck it over the top!

One baguette can go a surprisingly long way and is great with pretty much every pasta sauce dish. Just double the ingredients you need, serve smaller portions on to four plates and break the garlic bread into four large sections… voila, you've just fed more people!

Stir fry's

Almost every supermarket will have a discounted area where you can buy meat, vegetables, dairy products, and often some desserts for a ridiculously cheap price throughout the day. These areas are especially great at the end of the day (about 40 minutes before closing) when prices are slashed down, and are REAL bargains!

You can stir fry just about any vegetable, the secret of a good stir fry at this point in your student career, is to chop vegetables into the smallest size possible - especially things like broccoli and cauliflower. For stir fry's, we prefer our vegetables cut long and thin, not diced as we've explained in previous recipes!

Visit the reduced section in the supermarket and see what you can find! Precooked and uncooked chicken pieces, bits of bacon, pork chops, bits of fish, prawns (eat the same day) onions, red, yellow or green peppers, chard, cabbage, broccoli, courgette, carrots, you'll typically always find bean sprouts for a bargain price, as they go off quickly!

Before you start your stir fry, literally everything has to be chopped. Start with the meat or fish if you've got some. (If you're vegan or vegetarian, just leave the meat out and replace with extra veg, pulses, soya etc.) Slice meat into super thin strips half the thickness of a pencil and about 3 - 5 cm's long.

Put the meat on a separate dish to your vegetables, you'll want to cook this first. Next chop up all your vegetables, again into small strips about the ½ the thickness of a pencil and not too long.

Grab a frying pan (or wok), pour a spoon full of oil into this, add your meat and ½ an onion (optional). As you are frying the meat, add a spoonful of lazy garlic or garlic puree. Keep cooking until the meat turns brown and slightly crispy.

Next add your vegetables. Root vegetables (things like carrots) take lots longer than courgettes, peppers or cabbage. So put carrots in next if you have them.

Stir around the frying pan or the wok with the meat for 4 - 5 minutes, until if you shove your fork in a piece of carrot, it goes slightly droopy at the end.

Chuck in the rest of your vegetables. Turn up your heat and stir around the pan quickly. Some of the world's greatest chefs would do their nut with this approach... but hell... they are not students, and they're not here and frankly, it's still going to taste just as great. The vegetables should be sizzling in the pan (try not to let them stick).

When all the mixture is really hot and sizzling tip out of a pan and shove on your plate AND EAT!

TOP BANTS TOP TIP

If the prawns are pink - this means they're cooked already, so you don't need to pop them into the pan until the last two minutes of cooking - i.e. when the pan is sizzling hot. If the prawns are grey, add them at the start of the cooking process. ALWAYS use prawns the same day as you bought them, and never freeze them - it's just not worth the risk!

How to make Fried Chicken at home - A top Top Bants recipe!

Ingredients

Chicken cut into small pieces (about the size you'd find in a fried chicken restaurant or smaller)
1 egg for every 4 pieces of chicken (without the shell, broken into a bowl and mixed up)
2 cups of any kind of flour
2 - 4 teaspoons of curry powder
1 stock cube
2-3 teaspoons of ground pepper
½ teaspoon of salt (optional)
If you like spice – chuck a few teaspoons of chilli powder in for that extra heat!

Preparation

For the adventurous chefs amongst you, we have an easy tried and tested recipe. We love it so much we've cooked it many times now, and so we're going to explain in the easiest way possible.

Get some chicken! It doesn't matter if it's a whole chicken, chicken breasts, chicken wings (not at all expensive to buy in the supermarket) just chicken that's not been marinated.

Cut it up into little bits

Into a bowl, pop the flour, finely broken up stock cube, curry powder, pepper and salt, and stir it around.

Cover the chicken with the raw egg mixture.

If you have some cornflakes (or oats), you can mush these up and put them in too… or in fact just leave them whole for extra crispiness!

Take the chicken out of the egg mixture and cover completely in the flour mixture. You can do this either once or twice for an extra thick coating!

Get a frying pan, and fill it about ¾ of a cm with oil, but ensure it's less than ¼ full.

Bring the oil up to heat so that if you drop a bit of the egg mixture in it, it sizzles.

Carefully (using a spoon and fork) put the chicken into the oil mixture, ensuring the oil doesn't come more than half way up the pan, you may have to do this in stages.

Cook for just a few minutes on both sides until the flour mixture is all covered in oil, it will already start to resemble your favorite restaurant chicken!

Take the chicken out of the pan, and put on an oven proof tray. Bake in the oven for 30 - 40 minutes. Don't forget this part!

VOILA!

Vegetarian option. Replace the chicken with strips of soya, or vegetables follow the same recipe but cook for just 10 minutes in the oven.

How to eat when you are completely broke!

First off… somehow, there's pretty much always some money somewhere;

- Step one - go through the pockets of your clothes in your laundry basket.
- Step two - go through your coat pockets, paying special attention to the inside pockets.
- Step three - check underneath and behind the bed.
- Step four - check pockets of the clothes that are scattered over your bedroom floor.
- Step five - remember that money you're saving for the launderette - raid it for £1.
- Step six - if you have a washing machine - open up the filter at the bottom and check for money, same for the tumble dryer. (Make sure you have put the washing machine on a drain cycle first though)!
- Step seven - we just need to get you £1, as just £1 will feed you for 3 - 4 days if we play our cards right!
- Step eight - empty out old bags, laptop bags, bags you take out clubbing, suitcases, stuff from home!
- Step nine - we're getting desperate now, check make up bags, wash bags in the bathroom, and randomly used bags you've stored underneath the sink.
- Step ten - Check under the fridge, and literally lift the sofa up, surely there'll be a few coins there! (Turn the sofa upside down if necessary).

If all else fails, it's time to call in a favour from your flat mates. Don't feel guilty about it they're going to benefit too. Invite them for dinner, and tell them you need an advanced donation of 80p - let them know it's a potluck dinner.

Your mission, find some food, any food!

Scour the cupboards, fridge and freezer first! What do you have? Some frozen veg? A random sausage? Some bits of bacon you froze and forgot about? An old can of unopened tuna? A tin of lentils? A random egg? A block of old cheese? Some sliced bread? A tin of condensed tomato soup?

Right let's look at what we have - Why not show the Top Bants team on Instagram, and we'll see what we can do with it #TopBants!

If you have, or can get access to a few different types of vegetables (fresh or frozen) you can make vegetable stew. Cook the veggies up with a stock cube or two, and a bit of seasoning like salt and pepper. If you have bits of pre cooked bacon or sausage you can add these to the stew too! Literally ANYTHING can go in a stew! Once cooked thicken with a few spoonful's of corn flour mixed with water.

Or

You still have rice or pasta left?

With the rice, you can make a super tasty egg fried rice. With the pasta, you can make a delicious tomato pasta dish. The great thing is, so long as you have food that's in date, you can cook up a meal with pretty much anything, and so on the next pages, we share our inspiration.

The Top Bants team have brainstormed their best "poverty recipes", most were sensible so we thought we'd share these.

Hannah
    "Ok, so I was super poor, it was the end of term, I went through the cupboards, I had a scraggy tin of condensed chicken soup, some random pasta and three mushrooms. I cut the mushrooms up and fried them, then I chucked the chicken soup on top and heated it up in the pan. I cooked the pasta and then mixed it all together shabam it was great"

"Oh I've also got an awesome omelet / Spanish tortilla kind of recipe…"
    "Hang on Hannah, we love that let's include this in a sec".

James
    "I'm ashamed to say it, but I once lived off of tomato curry with a fried egg on top for three days. I just had two tins of tomatoes, curry powder and rice. I mixed up the curry powder in some butter in a pan (no oil left) and made a curry paste. I chucked the tomatoes in and cooked it for about 10 minutes. Fried up an egg, and served it with rice."

Stephen
    "I'm always broke, my best one was a homemade 'Chinese soup in a cup' I got my soup cup mix out of the packet and made it. Then, I put it into a saucepan, got an egg, whisked it up and chucked it in and kept stirring. It was almost like the real thing you'd get in a Chinese restaurant, only I didn't have chicken soup, so it was like a minestrone one." #dontbelikestephen!

"Another time, I may have found a pan beside the sink with some food in it, well there was no sign telling me not to, so… I ate it" again #dontbelikestephen!

Emma
"Yeah, I'm always broke too, and I hate cooking. In my cupboard I found a mashed potato mix, I'm not even sure how it got there, but I made that with cheese on top, actually it wasn't bad."

Erin
"I'm all about pasta, and I've done the same as Emma, just with Pasta and cheese. If I've got a few spare veggies I'll throw them in."

Stephen
"Pineapple curry… that was my worst"
The team had to stop here and find out more…
"Well I thought it was a tin of tomatoes, but the label had come off, and I literally didn't have anything else, then I thought it could be ok, because you do have pineapple on pizza"

The Top Bants team has decided to exclude the rest of this conversation; due to the fact Stephen is beyond hope! #dontbelikestephen.

Hannah
"COUSCOUS! I had a 2 day old curry knocking around in the fridge. I heated it up and when it was warm, took it off the heat and added a cup of couscous! Left it for 10 minutes to absorb the juice! It was super delicious, and fed 2 of us!"

James

"My problem at uni was I never had time to think about cooking, so I'd make a big chilli at the weekend and then eat it through the week! However, by Friday, when I got sick of chilli. I'd cook a carbonara and this recipe HAS to be in the book!

James' quick and cheap Carbonara

Ingredients

1 tub of supermarkets own brand soft cheese. (Melt in a pan)
3 cups of cooked pasta
A handful of mushrooms, lardons or bits of bacon
Grated cheese
Ground black pepper.

Preparation

Cook the mushrooms, or lardons or bacon, or anything else (you can pop onions in the pan too)
Add the soft cheese, and stir until it's melted
Add the pasta to the mix (already cooked)
Add salt and pepper to taste

If James was feeling a bit flush or there was some cheese left in the fridge, he'd chop it up find and mix it into the pan at the end, just before serving.

Hannahs Omelet / Spanish tortilla thing.

Ingredients

So you can only do this if you have three eggs.

Look in the fridge for anything you have. Some onions, pre-cooked potatoes, a pepper or any other vegetable. (Just not tinned tomatoes)
Look in the freezer, get some frozen vegetables like broccoli. Just cook it all up and stick it in a colander to drain.
Any meat, (optional) like bits of bacon, bits of sausage. Make sure they're cooked.
Crack and mix up your eggs. Add a pinch of salt and pepper.
Preparation

So when the vegetables have been drained. Stick a little oil in your pan, and fry your meat and vegetables together.

Once they're cooking. Chuck in the seasoned egg mix.

Stir around the pan until the egg starts to form lumps but is still runny.

Stop stirring, turn the heat down and leave for 3 - 5 minutes.

For right handed people…

Get a plate (the same size or slightly bigger than the frying pan,) and put it on the top of the pan.

Hold the plate in place with your left hand. Hold the pan handle in your right hand, pick up the pan, and ensuring you have the plate in place turn the pan over, so that the mix comes out of the pan and onto the plate.

Slide the omelet / tortilla thing off of the plate back into the pan, so that the cooked bottom is at the top and the top is at the bottom. (The top should now be well cooked).

Put back on the heat and cook for a further few minutes. To check the bottom has cooked, pop the plate back on the top and tip over.

Some final Top Bants cooking tips

- Don't ever be afraid to experiment, just #dontbelikestephen!

- When you're following a recipe, unless it's a cake, or bread thing that needs flour, don't worry too much about quantities, it's just a guide to help you to know what needs to go in.

- Always make sure you stir things like casseroles and curries regularly, because otherwise they can stick to the bottom of the pan.

- If you burn your pan, don't throw it away. Get some washing powder, pop 3 spoonful's in the pan with a litre of water and cook it for 30 minutes, you'll usually find the burn comes off.

- Don't use metal things in non-stick pans (like frying pans) as you scratch the non-stick off the pan and it will no longer be non-stick (this can ruin your life).

- If you've made a casserole, stew or curry and it's a bit runny. Don't panic. You can either continue to cook for a bit longer until the water evaporates OR Get 2 teaspoons of corn flour, mix well with ½ a cup of water and tip it into the mix. Stir well whilst you bring your cooking up to the boil and you will find it thickens super quickly!

- If you've made a curry and it's too spicy, chuck some natural yoghurt in it to "cool the spice off".

- If you've made a chili, and it's super strong, chuck a spoonful of sugar into it to dampen down the spiciness!

- Some recipes are in oz (ounces) and lb (pounds), some in kg (kilograms)and gr grams, and some are measured by the cup or spoon... how do we work with that? For now, just Google it, and in Top Bants in the kitchen we'll give you some quick hacks!

- Always be careful adding salt, pepper and spices. We've all been caught out on many occasions, taste the dish several times during cooking and add flavouring a little at a time.

- Just bought to our attention, literally days before the final edit, was the shelf life of food. If you've opened and only used ½ a tin. Pop the remains in the bowl and cover them up. They will be good to eat and cook with for another two days! So time for that omelette, or chuck them in a stir fry or curry.

- Always check the use by date on meat items, and stick with them. If you think your meat is slightly off, or your fridge isn't working properly, take it out and smell it. If in doubt... chuck it out.

Recipies from Home!

Make sure to bring some recipes from home and pop them here.
Don't forget to tag us too with your recipe inspirations!

Washing dishes

The Top Bants team knows that you know how to wash dishes. We're going to give you a few top tips here though in how to make this process as painless as possible and tips about how to survive if you run out of washing up liquid, or your sponge looks like it's storing a zillion bacteria and really needs to be replaced… but of course… you don't have any money!

It's a sad fact of life that dishes need washing from time to time. To reduce infection, to minimise the likelihood of food poisoning and to ensure your flat mates stay friends with you and you don't all fall out!

The key to washing up is to do it straight away. It's not as tedious as it sounds, after all, you're not clearing up after your entire family. It's simply the cooking things you've used, a plate, fork and knife - how hard can this be!

TOP BANTS TOP TIP

It's much harder to wash up dishes with dried food spanning back several days or even weeks than it is to wash up a plate and utensils you've just used.

Dried food on plates takes more scrubbing, more washing up liquid and more procrastinating time. So just do the dishes when you've used them and not when you need them!

<u>Running out of washing up liquid.</u>

It's an inevitable consequence that the washing up liquid is going to run out at some time and BINGO, there's yours and everyone else's excuse not to do the washing up. It's a wise move to agree on the washing up liquid debate PRIOR to it running out. As there are several benefits to having it!

Without it you won't wash up, your housemates won't wash up, there'll be no cooking facilities, or clean plates, or mugs, or cutlery for that matter. There'll just be this one heaving mass of dried up moldy plates in the bowl that no one wants to go near to or indeed to touch. Matters then get much worse, with no plates or means of cooking you all end up living off of a diet of biscuits, ready-made sandwiches and crisps. This all eats really quickly and quite drastically into your meager living budget.

Finally, things get so bad that you have to stop inviting friends around as you can't even offer coffee and you're too embarrassed to go into your kitchen. The final turn of events will come when the latest love of your life comes into discover the catastrophic series of events in the sink and finishes with you. Or parents come for an impromptu visit to take you out for lunch, but stumble across the nightmare in the kitchen, spend their whole time clearing it up for you, and then buying you goods to keep you going for another few weeks... bang goes lunch at your favourite local eatery!

Keeping on top of the washing up is a win win situation for all. It costs less than £1 for a bottle of washing up liquid and whilst it's a lot of money on a tight budget it's a worthwhile long term investment. Shared between 3 - 4 of you, it's actually very little.

One final note… whilst we're on the washing up pile, there is a whole political issue that comes into play when piles of washing up aren't done, leaving feelings of either mild resentment to utter hatred! We want to avoid this; we want to live a calm and peaceful existence amongst our housemates so take it from the Top Bants team. Keep on top of your washing up as a minimum but better still, if there are some plates or pans in the washing up bowl that you clearly have to move before you can wash up your own items, then win extra points by washing them up whilst moving them out of the way!

TOP BANTS TOP TIP

Casual discussions in the kitchen on organising cleaning rotas, or putting up polite signs are super effective, try to avoid some kind of confrontational meeting where blame is chucked around the room, and try to gain agreement early on in the process to ensure everyone is on board with keeping the kitchen clean!

ANOTHER TOP BANTS TOP TIP

When all else fails, you have no washing up liquid, and no means of buying any, use a bit of cheap shampoo.

Tea towels

Tea towels are supposed to be used to dry up dishes. This means you don't have to leave stuff on the draining board, and you can put it away to clear the kitchen for others.

They are not a hand drying receptacle!

They harbour HEAPS of germs, as just about everyone will use them to dry their hands, leave them wet on the kitchen counter, and also use them for mopping up all sorts of student "juice".

WASH YOUR TEA TOWEL REGULARLY. We're talking a minimum of once a week. You may (as boring as it sounds) find it handy to have several tea towels stacked away for future use in the kitchen.

Chapter 6

Top Bants on Washing Clothes, Stains and Collateral Damage

Using a washing machine / visiting the launderette.

For the uninitiated a launderette is a place where you go to get your clothes washed and cleaned. You can find launderettes that do a service wash (where you dump your bag on someone who works there and pick it up clean, folded and dry - more expensive than the hands on approach to washing) or a do it yourself launderette, or both. The launderette is a large room like a shop where you will find machines scattered around the edge of the room. These are typically washing machines (you use these first), spinners (where you spin wet clothes) and, dryers (cost you a fortune to use, but essential to dry the clothes you've been recycling for the past month or two). You will typically find "folding tables" (or areas) in the launderette. These are handy for shoving piles of your clean clothes on before you fold them up and take them home.

In addition to these things provided by the launderette company you will often find lost items of clothing, magazines and newspapers, discarded food morsels and a delightful array of other peoples misplaced "stuff".

As tempting as it may be to shove all your washing into a large bin bag, and take it home for mum every month or so, there will be regular times when your washing is piled so high, or it's so stinky, that frankly, it's time to embrace the beauty of the launderette.

Launderettes can be pretty cool places too, YouTube the 'Levi launderette' ad from the 80's, we are not guaranteeing yours will be the same experience but, who knows.

TOP BANTS TOP TIP

Visit a cheap shop, and stock up on 20 pairs of underwear and socks (all the same colour). This way you have at least 20 days of supplies. Bikini bottoms can also double up as underwear. Boys, turning your underwear inside out and using it sideways really does NOT give you 6 days of wear from your undies!

Where to find your friendly launderette.

Lots of student halls have launderettes attached to them, however, in many cases, they can be more expensive than normal launderettes.

Google is your friend. Locate several different local launderettes, often Google will have a web page for them, including a little graph which will tell you it's busiest times, avoid times when it receives a lot of traffic, as you'll have to wait for ages for a machine. Frankly, life's too short!

When looking at the Google reviews, you'll find it often has higher star ratings because it has a dispensary for washing powder.

TOP BANTS TOP TIP

Buy your washing powder/conditioner from a low cost supermarket chain, it's far cheaper! For those of you feeling homesick, buy something mum and dad use, as it will remind you of home. If you have limited space, buy capsules, easier to store, and cart to the launderette.

Stephen shoves cheap washing powder in one of his socks, which he takes in his laundry bag and chucks in the machine. This is such a great idea and keeps costs low. Thank you!

Before your first official laundry visit, find out what coins the machines take, get yourself a jar, (recycled peanut butter jar / coffee jar) and every time you have a spare 20p/50p/£1, pop them in the jar to ensure you always have spare money for clean clothes! Always make sure you take more than enough money for your first trip, wet clothes and clothes that aren't completely dry start to smell really quickly!

Student launderettes, and large commercial ones, now run from an app from your phone. Be careful here, remember every penny counts. Shop around for the cheapest launderette and ensure those apps are safe.

- There are certain things that make this whole experience more enjoyable. Firstly, take a friend. There are many reasons for this.
- It's a great way to bond with new friends in halls and from your course.
- Save money by combining your white clothes and lighter coloured clothes into one machine, and your dark clothes (like jeans and dark t-shirts and jumpers) in another.
- Use your friend to guard the machine you're taking your clothes out of, so no one can push in before you've emptied it.
- Use your friend to shotgun the dryers, and stand in front of an empty one before anyone jumps the queue!

- Be careful to follow instructions carefully when using an app or card scanning device, as some of us have scanned whilst the machine is open, meaning we get charged twice for the wash.

Things that come out quite wet

Launderettes are renowned for having machines that don't drain and spin clothes well. Don't panic. Most of them have spinning machines, and its good economy to use either them, or the extra fast spin cycle on the machine.

TOP BANTS TOP TIP

Spend the money on the spinner as the dryer the clothes are when they go into the tumble dryers, the cheaper the whole process will be - dryers are money eaters, spinners are your friend!

Ensure that all your washing is in the machine before it starts. Some machines us students used in London reset if we had to open the door, and we were charged twice on our app.

Certainly the first time you go to a launderette, you won't know how long the machines take, and it's worth staying around to ensure no one steals your clothes. Take a book or some study material with you so that you can keep an eye on what's going on.

Other advantages of launderettes… they are usually pretty warm places and unless someone is processing a local rugby clubs kit they smell pretty good. Launderettes are a great place to go on a hangover as they're great to sleep in, they're fun places to people watch, meet new friends, and if you're lucky they'll have Wi-Fi. So they can double up as a library or just a place to indulge in catching up on social media.

Not only that, but you can even impress your grandparents who will undoubtedly be worried by the fact you've left the nest, and often, because you're so busy partying and studying, it's hard to find time to catch up with them.

Launderettes are typically quite places, and great to make a call to older family members. Not only will it impress them that you're in the launderette, it gives them something to talk about with their local friends! Trust us, they'll be impressed.

What do all those signs mean on your washing labels?

If you have a symbol with a hand on it avoid washing this like the plague! This means your clothes are really fragile and most likely made of wool or some sensitive material. The hand means hand wash only! This is a really tiresome activity.

On the next page, we've created a handy little graphic that will help you to check your labels and decide what to do.

TOP BANTS TOP TIP

Wash new coloured clothes on their own for the first time as, often, the dye will come out. When doing a wash, if possible, wash coloured clothes together on a cooler wash, and white clothes separately to coloured clothes. So long as your clothes have been washed before (preferably several times) you are usually pretty safe to chuck them all into a cool quick wash together (try to use a temperature less than 40 degrees)

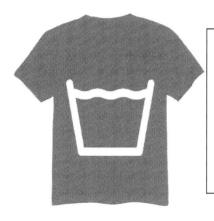

Ok so this symbol is great! It means you can wash the item (always handy).
Stephen from our team thought it was some kind of drink #dontbelikestephen!

When you see this label with a number on, it shows you the maximum temperature you can wash your clothes at in the machine. Most things wash safely at 40.

BE WARNED!

This label means "Hand Wash Only".
Do not pop these clothes in the machine if you can possibly help it.
You have been warned!

We're still not sure why this label exists, as it means "Do Not Wash"

Please try to wash your clothes regularly. If your clothes have this label, consult a dry cleaner for information.

This means "Dry Clean only" which is a very expensive way to get your clothes clean.
If washed in a machine it's likely to lose its shape, or worse case, to fall apart!

Using a tumble dryer.

Tumble dryers are used for drying your clothes after they have been washed and you have put them in the spinner if necessary.

As we previously mentioned, you want to make sure your clothes have been well spun in the washing machine, as the wetter they are when they go in, the longer they will take to dry, and the more it will cost you.

If possible, find a regular launderette visitor and ask their opinion as to how long the clothes should be in the tumble dryer. Typically aim for an hour. Some materials take a shorter time to dry than others. When you think they should be done, open the door and let the clothes cool a bit. If they still feel damp to the touch, pop them on for another 15 minutes.

Check the dryer after about half an hour. If some clothes feel dry, take them out of the machine and start folding them. This way, the clothes inside the dryer will dry quicker, and save you more money!

TOP BANTS TOP TIP

Dryers don't give you your money back if you haven't spent it, so don't overload it with money, open and check the dryer regularly.

What to do if your clothes are creased?

Well, of course, you could iron them, but we just don't have the time or inclination for this!
Get a coat hanger (given free at most clothes shops and you can often find free ones in charity shops, and also of course, back at home), if you don't have one, borrow one from someone. Hang the item of clothing from the shower rail or towel rail in the bathroom. Make sure you have a hot and steamy shower or bath and the steam will get the creases out!

Collateral Damage - accidents, stains and other disasters

As we all know accidents happen and as we all also know more accidents happen when alcohol is involved. And so here is your essential guide for accident induced stains that can seriously ruin your clothes or reduce the amount returned on your house deposit! OK, before we start on the detail, there are a couple of points to remember regarding stains;

- Get onto stains as quickly as possible.
- If possible don't let them dry out.
- With clothes, don't wash and dry them first as this process will set the stain colour forever.
- Don't rub over a large area with lots of liquid as this can often spread the stain, blot the stained area and add liquids sparingly.

How to get stains out of clothes, from carpets and off of walls...

TOP BANTS TOP TIP

> Beer and white wine are your friends for many stains! Yes, we know you'd rather drink it, but it has some surprising cleaning properties, and can help you get rid of stains, so always useful to keep a ready supply in your fridge, either as a useful cleaner, or… simply a pre-drink!

Coffee and tea stains in the carpet or on your favourite white top?

Act quickly, and while the stain is still wet. Just pop to the fridge and get that beer out. Pour over the stain, rub the beer lightly over the area, and soak up with kitchen towel, or loo roll.

Don't rub the towel or loo roll, just place it over the top of the beer, and push down towards the stain, (otherwise you'll get bits of tissue mixed in with the stain). Repeat several times until the stain has gone, and then wash with water.

Red wine stains

Red wine is a nightmare to get out, and a red wine spill is an inevitable consequence of being a student.

When buying red wine, always buy a bottle of white, mainly, because it takes ages to go off if you keep it in the fridge, and if you get the screw top version you can have the occasional glass without feeling as if you've overindulged.

If you spill red wine down your new white top, or worse still, on a carpet don't despair!
Grab the white wine out of the fridge and pour on top of the stain. Blot the area i.e. place the cloth, push down but don't rub, repeat again until the red wine has almost gone. Pour salt over the area and vacuum up the salt after 1 minute.

Do not leave the salt on overnight, as it can bleach the carpet. (Trust us, we know)!

Getting ketchup out of the carpet and off the walls.

If you spill ketchup, you have to act quickly, because once it dries, it's almost impossible to remove the stain! First off... do NOT rub the ketchup, it will mix with the fibers of the carpet and be a nightmare to remove.

Get a knife from the kitchen, and carefully scrape the ketchup off of the carpet. Next get some salt, and sprinkle over the stain, leave the salt on the stain for 10 minutes and then hoover up.

You will probably find some ketchup colour still in the carpet, if you do, get ½ cup of washing powder or liquid, and mix with ½ cup of water. Pour over the stain, and leave for 10 minutes.

Slowly massage the stain and blot up the excess liquid. Repeat several times if necessary. NOTE - do not scrub the wall, or the paint/wall paper may come off, just dab the cleaning mixture onto the wall.

Alternatively, if you have white wine vinegar (as recommended in the cupboard essentials), work the neat vinegar into the stain, and you should find it comes off!

Getting sick off of the carpet.

Let's face it, if you're not sick on someone's carpet in the next few years of your university life you're simply not trying hard enough!

TOP BANTS TOP TIP

> It's really important to keep an eye on someone who is vomiting, as they can easily choke on it if they're really drunk. Stay with the voming person and, as they try to sleep, make them lie on their side to avoid choking. If the person seems very ill as a result of vomiting, or becomes unconscious and unresponsive, call the emergency services.

First off, let's consider what we can do to avoid sick on the carpet in the first place! If you or a friend are feeling sick and you're in the house the first place to attempt to get to is a toilet. Bathrooms (especially student bathrooms) are far easier to clean, than a bedroom carpet!

Other items that can potentially catch vomit, and minimise the disaster include, a pre-designated sick bucket, a saucepan, a bin bag, a laundry basket, a mop bucket (preferably empty) a hoodie, a carrier bag from the supermarket, a pillowcase (to catch the lumps). We recommend not 'vomming' out of the window as you could fall or chunder on a passerby, or upset your landlord who will have vomit to clear up from your garden the following morning, not to mention the inevitable stain down the wall, which can literally take years, and lots of expense, to remove. (Trust us here; the Top Bants team has experienced MOST of these events, with the exception of falling out of the window).

A fascinating thing about chunder is no matter what you've eaten, or even if you've not eaten at all, there are always chunks in it, if you can somehow catch the chunks you're off to a good start!

So, let's face it, there are going to be times when no matter what our best intentions are someone chunders on the carpet and someone else, perhaps you, is going to have to clean it up.

Start with the lumps; once the lumps are gone the rest becomes easy well, easier!

TOP BANTS TOP TIP

There's always that one person at uni who likes cleaning and for some reason they are happy to be the nominated "chunder cleaner". Make friends with this person, invite them to dinner, lend them your clothes (they'll always come back cleaner) and, remember, these people will be the organised people who happen to own cleaning liquid, cloths and detergent.

<u>Getting rid of chunder chunks.</u>

Grab an old plastic bag or bin bag. If you have a dustpan (as recommended in essentials) put the bag over the dustpan. Use this as a handy scoop to get the lumps up. In the event you don't have a dustpan, get the bag and check there are no holes in it. Turn the bag inside out, put your hands inside and scoop up the lumps.

Use tissue or kitchen roll to blot most of the moisture up. Put used tissues and kitchen roll into the plastic bag with the lumpy sick in it. Once you have removed all lumps, and fibrous bits pour on your detergent mixture or better still, ½ a cup of white wine vinegar.

Gently massage the cleaning mixture into the carpet. Blot the area with toilet roll or kitchen roll and re-apply cleaning mixture. Repeat the exercise until the area is clean!

<u>Getting sick off the walls.</u>

The first point to note is don't ever be tempted to hide sick on walls by relocating sofas or beds as it will still be there the next day, or indeed months later. It's always better to clean up sick whilst it's wet. Follow the steps as above. Blot walls (don't rub) with detergent mixture.

<u>Mattresses</u>.

It's a really great deal for landlords to charge for mattress stains, some of the Top Bants team have been charged up to £200 for a replacement mattress, so first rule of being a student is to check your mattress from the start! Top, bottom and sides. If there are stains on it take photos immediately and inform your landlord by email with attached photos of the stains.

The first really cool thing to know is that in most student housing, halls, furnished flats, and most holiday hosting properties have "Mattress protectors". It's like a sheet that sits between your sheet and a mattress and aims to keep the mattress clean and to last longer. Often the protector is zipped up over the mattress.

Take photos of any stains on the mattress protector then unzip it, take it off and inspect your mattress. If it's clean and, parents / grandparents would be happy, then that's fine. If you find even the slightest stain, again take a photo and report it immediately or, trust us, you will be charged for it! Again, we speak from experience at the Top Bants HQ!

When you move into your student accommodation, always check the mattress has a protector, and if it doesn't then its good economy to buy one. After a spillage, If you can get the mattress protector off of the mattress pretty quickly you can wash and replace and nobody will be any the wiser.

However, there will be times when things are spilt, and no matter how quick you are, the stain will go through to the mattress. Try to get these stains whilst fresh, as it's far easier to remove them.

Make up a detergent mix, ½ detergent and ½ water; pour over the stain and scrub. Blot excess water from the mattress, and repeat until clean. Try to choose a warm day and dry your mattress in the sun by the window or beside a radiator.

How to get chewing gum out of clothing

Euck! Chewing gum on your clothes. Don't panic, here's a sure fire way to get it out. For this you'll need a plastic bag and a freezer. Pop the garment into a plastic bag with the chewing gum facing the outside. You really want the chewing gum to freeze so pop it in the freezer for 2 - 3 hours.

Once frozen, take the garment out of the bag and with a blunt kitchen knife peel the gum off of the clothing as quickly as possible. If the gum defrosts pop it back into bag and into the freezer for another two hours, and repeat.

Chapter 7

When you host a party!

Let's face it we ALL love a good party and most especially the Top Bants team! However, there's something really terrifying about hosting your own party. It brings back memories of mum and dad returning home 2 hours earlier than they promised, the tins in the kitchen cupboard being relieved of their labels so the parents didn't know if they were cooking up custard or cat food, the discovery of condoms in most unsuitable places, or the discovery of half-naked bodies in your parents en suite! Not to mention the bag of sick neatly hidden in the airing cupboard that doesn't get discovered until a week after the party! Yes, we've all been there, and even your parents have! Don't forget to tag #TopBants with your before, during and after party photos!

Living away from home for the first time is simply the best, finally you get to party until the late hours of the morning, you don't have to worry about being caught in various states of undress, or moving the rug in the lounge to cover up the vomit stains. All of a sudden, it just seems like a wonderful idea to throw unlimited parties and invite goodness knows who to come and eat your food, drink your booze and trash your place instead of theirs!

Now, the sensible side of the Top Bants team says, "Don't put yourself through this," simply go to other people's parties! It costs less, there's no mess to clean up, no neighbours to worry about and no damage!?!

You're not going to listen hey! But #dontbelikestephen!

Let's minimise the inevitable damage to this by considering a few fundamentals. Who are you going to invite? Start off by just inviting people in your halls. If they've been invited they can't complain about the loud music, they don't have far to come, or indeed to go home at the end of the night. Even if you don't know them you know where to find them and, if you meet some really lovely ones they may come back and help with the clearing up the next day.

People from your halls are less likely to bring souvenirs they found on their way to your party like, for example, the car park barrier they dismantled and found hanging out of your bedroom window the next day (thanks for that tale Stephen) or the cones with the lights on and, worst case, if they do bring them it's not so far for you to go to deliver them back to the gifter!

TOP BANTS TOP TIP

BYOD, BYOB, BYOA, or simply BYO. Always advertise the party as a "bring your own" drink. Even if you are supplying some alcohol, it is the norm and completely standard for fellow students to bring their own booze! The party will be no worse, and simply won't cost you the earth. DO ENSURE however that you declare it's a BYO prior to the party!

Advertising your party on social media;

We've all read the horror stories of crowds of locals turning up uninvited to a party. You know your Social Media, you've all had the talk in school, as fun and exciting as it is to throw a ridiculously large party, and get to know heaps of strangers… we suggest you don't do this to yourself! #dontbelikestephen!

Snacks

It's reasonable to chuck some snacks, crisps, nuts, olives out for the party but, they'll be gone pretty much immediately. Hide the snacks in a cupboard and bring them out gradually through the night to ensure latecomers have something to munch on!

Get a few loaves of bread in. The more drunk your fellow students get the more they'll want sobering up with toast and marmite/jam or that elusive jar of pate that mum and dad bought smells of cat food, now is the time to crack it open!

Speakers

There's always going to be that one person in halls who, no matter how lovely you are to them, will just not want to join you. That's fine; however, it's important to be respectful to your neighbours. By all means get a big loud speaker, but minimise its external volume.

TOP BANTS TOP TIP

By popping your speaker on a big old armchair, a mattress or on a sit on bean bag. The sound will still be the same, but it will travel less through the building!

Vom receptacles

Always a good one! Empty the bin before everyone gets there, and pop in a new bin bag. This way if someone pukes in the bin, it's easy enough to clear out. Same goes for mop buckets, always remove the mop. As most of your fellow hall residents can read, it's often quite handy to stick a well-placed sign on the bucket (just so they know).

Plates, cups and mopping facilities

The Top Bants team is all for reducing the effects of plastic on our world, so paper plates (if you're serving food). Better still serve finger food or get them to bring their own plates and glasses)

Paper cups can be handy (to save on washing up) and don't forget to borrow mopping facilities if you don't have them!

TOP BANTS TOP TIP

Advice is to buy a few kitchen rolls from a super cheap store. Leaving them around in easy to reach places! Sadly, we don't recommend loo rolls, as there's always that one person who has been running out of loo roll for days and will simply pop one in their bag, Kitchen roll is far bigger and less likely to "go missing" it also leaves less of a mess than a well rubbed piece of loo roll on a carpet! Remember, blot don't rub!

Chapter 8

Top Bants on Saving Money

EBay is your friend... and other sales stories

Looking for a dress or suit for the next ball? Or just a fancy dress costume.

Scour the charity shops, it's free entertainment if nothing else, and you'll always find something you never knew you needed. Better still, you could find things for a bargain price that you can sell at a profit on eBay! One of our TopBants team found a £700 pair of shoes for £2 in a charity shop recently, they went straight on eBay, and the profit paid for her summer holiday!

As mentioned previously try searching "free" on Gumtree... we could actually kit out your entire life - always have a look locally to you, we've even found a free car with one months MOT! We've found bikes, computer screens, if only we needed more stuff in the office here! Don't think about this as being freeloaders, think of it as upcycling, better still you can either upgrade it and sell it on if you're super broke, or give it to the next needy student!

We've just run a search on EBay for some designer dresses, and just for fun have misspelt designer names. Have a look for yourselves. Through our search, we located some cool ball gowns that were selling for approximately £300, however, by just changing one or two characters of the designers name we found exactly the same ball gown for £34. So watch out for bad spelling, it could bring you some bargains!

On a final note… we know you're only going to wear "That Dress" once! Top Bants advice… if you're going to go for that "designer dress" get it from eBay, wear it, get some stunning photos of it (i.e. not on a hanger) get it professionally washed, and pop it back on eBay.

A well-presented dress will sell for more, and if well listed too, you could get more for it than you paid!

One of the Top Bants team uses this method to pay for all of her clothes. Literally buying and selling dresses on eBay, and funding her rather expensive designer kit!

Getting other stuff for free or reducing your costs!

One of our team just got a job working in The City. Having just finished uni, and just setting up home he literally couldn't afford the basics. In one quick trip to a well-known cafe, we procured for him our spare sugar sachets and extra tissues to save him buying toilet roll! We even grabbed a few of the little milk containers that were unopened so he could have milk with his coffee in the morning!

Yes it did cost a cappuccino, but that was the Editors shout, so doesn't count.

Get a funky water bottle

Water from the tap is free!

Take a packed lunch

We all love to eat out but, frankly as a student, it's just wonderful to be able to eat. Packed lunches needn't be just sandwiches and a packet of crisps. Leftover pasta from last night is always a winner, as is couscous. Stephen recommends not taking curry in your lunch box - we wonder why! Nor, he says raw onions. But getting into the habit of taking a lunch box filled with yummy home cooked food will save you a fortune!

Buy second hand books

Six of us have just reevaluated our reading lists.

Hannah	Read two books.
Stephen	Didn't buy any! (No surprise there).
James	Bought them all but, never read a single one.
Emma B	Bought them all (because she thought she had to) but, only used the colouring in anatomy book which she coloured in when her parents cancelled their Netflix subscription one night without telling her.
Beth	Got them from older students via social media (less than half price).
Erin	Bought them new, read a few, sold them on to a younger student.

Do you REALLY need these books? If so, join some social media groups for the years above you. Guaranteed they'll be selling unopened copies that you can buy for a reasonable price!

Look to change your mobile phone provider

Who pays your mobile subscription and what's in your package? What do you need and what don't you need?

Keep your eyes peeled for student deals, and look our regularly to chop and change your contract depending on the deals available at the time.

TOP BANTS TOP TIP

Don't tie yourself into a long term contract of over a year. It's usually cheaper too to get a phone separate to your contract, so shop around!

Chapter 9

Top Bants on surviving the excesses of student life

Embarking on student life can be quite daunting, and often intimidating. First things first, we have literally all been there. Two of our team don't drink at all, and were worried how this would be construed by their peers. #dontbelikestephen!

There are literally so many activities you can throw yourself into as a student, which do NOT involve alcohol and we recommend you involve yourself as much as you possibly can in these.

- because it's cheaper
- because it's safer
- because it's cooler
- because, you are at university after all to study
- because you don't want to be like Stephen #dontbelikestephen!

However, we also understand that it's possibly, your first time away from home, and we recognise that during freshers weeks, many university activities revolve around a drinking culture.

NOTE… you can honestly have heaps of fun, without partying until the late hours of the day, or early hours of the morning! If you choose to, then please do pace yourself, and don't be dragged into the drinking culture.

If you do drink however, keep reading this chapter!

Predrinks

Drinking out is an 'OH so expensive' experience and a massive cause of greater student debt! So, this is why the "predrink" culture is so alive and kicking at uni! You'll not want to be warned about the perils of mixing drinks, drinking to excess and the damage it can do to your liver, so on that note, we won't because after all you can 'Google' it!

TOP BANTS TOP TIPS

Milk thistle is good for the liver; it comes in tablet and diluted form from most health stores. Get a stack and, before you go out for the night, just have one! They're natural; they won't do you any harm at all!

Water and food before your night out

We speak from experience that it's an exceptionally bad idea to drink on an empty stomach. Not only are you at risk from feeling decidedly ill through the night and possibly the next morning but also reduce the aftermath of a less than sober night. We want to reduce ways in which you're likely to end up messaging your ex., or worst still, meeting up with them (remember… they're an ex. for a reason)! There are a host of other reasons why it's a great idea to prepare sensibly for a night out and to reduce your alcohol consumption. Here are just a few reasons to prepare your body for a night out as experienced first-hand from the Top Bants team; Remember, over and above all #dontbelikestephen!

- You'll miss the fun if you peak too early;
- Your body will feel so much better in the morning for a night of relative sobriety;

- You'll remember what an awesome night out you had;
- You won't have alcohol poisoning;
- You'll find yourself in your own bed with only your own name to remember - it's always more comfy and there's a lot less angst involved;
- You won't wake up in a hospital corridor with your dad there;
- You won't have embarrassing videos to watch over social media;
- You won't be poor - alcohol makes you very poor;
- You can be that friend that everyone goes to for help;
- You won't tell your best friend, who you've been lusting after for years, how much you truly love them; (Hey Tori)
- You can be that special friend that holds a random strangers hair back whilst they chunder;
- You won't wake up in a toilet;
- You'll be on time for lectures the next day (let's remember how much you're paying for them);
- You won't waste a weekend! So many fun things to be done at the weekend;
- You won't wake up with a kebab stuck to your ear, or permanent marker pen on your face;
- You won't be the centre of a drama! Who was it that said "Alcohol is dramas best friend" it's true;
- You're more likely to get hold of a safe taxi company, or remember how to get home safely;

- You're less likely to lose your friends in a club;
- You won't step into a pile of well positioned chunder when you get out of bed in the morning;
- You're less likely to upset your friends or end up with your friends boyfriend/girlfriend;
- You're less likely to wake up with random bruises and scars;
- You'll be able to keep your breakfast down the next morning;
- You won't feel like shit tomorrow.

We cannot tell you enough about the value of water to your system. We are after all "What we eat, and drink" and we really don't want you to leave uni looking like a cross between a vodka bottle and a packet of crisps!

TOP BANTS TOP TIP

Line your stomachs before you go out, something with slow release carbs and fats! Drink a pint of water before you leave that way you'll drink slower to start with.

For every drink you have through the night, drink the same volume of water!

Before you go out pop a large glass of water beside your bed. That way it will be there in the night when you need it.

Hangovers, cures and loving your liver

We just wish there was the ultimate hangover cure out there; most of the Top Bants team have tried them all. Everything from packets of "goodness" bought from a chemist to "hair of the dog" We don't recommend drinking your way through the following day.

The best way to avoid a hangover of course is not to drink in the first place - like you're going to listen to us hey! Alternatively, you could just have a small glass or two of your favourite drink, or make your drink last through the night. Well actually... it could!

The Top Bants team have been known to make a beer or glass of wine last all evening, especially when they have a full day ahead of them the next day, but realistically, there are some (not many) of you who are going to wake up with a hangover at some point during your university career.

Below, we've written a few of our own (non-science based) ideas that the Top Bants team have tried and tested!

First of all, we need to understand what a hangover actually is, and identify if you have one!
Ask yourself the following;

- Did you drink last night?
- Have you been drunk in the last 24 hours?
- Are you feeling like your head is pounding?
- Is your mouth feeling really dry?
- Was the room spinning last night when you went to bed?
- Is the room still spinning?

- Have you chundered in the last 24 hours as a result of excess alcohol?
- Does everything hurt in your body?
- Do you have the most raging headache?
- Do you just want to go back to bed and spend the day there?
- Are you feeling anxious or weepy?
- Is your face puffy?
- Is there little to no brain function?
- Have you got random and unexplained bruises?

If you have answered yes to questions one or two, and yes to at least two of the following questions, then it's a sad fact of life that you're most likely to be hung-over!

TOP BANTS TOP TIP

If you haven't been drunk, and you feel like this, it could be a good idea to take your health seriously, you could have a virus, Freshers flu, or some general bug. If it persists, and your temperature is high, perhaps consider seeing a professional.

A final note on hangovers;
People of East Asian origin watch out - though we probably don't need to tell you! If you are of East Asian origin it's a fact that you're most likely not able to cope with alcohol really at all. This is due to a mutation in the genes for the enzyme alcohol dehydrogenase. If you're of East Asian descent you will most likely be aware of this and the Asian flush you get after just a tiny amount of alcohol! If you're drinking with a person of East Asian descent, be aware that they are most likely familiar with the problem of 'Asian Flush', keep an eye on them. Don't encourage them to keep up to your drinking speed!

Chapter 10

Top Bants on Health, Happiness and Keeping Safe

Let's face it, no matter how independent or not you are, the change from having everything on tap at home to looking after yourself at uni can be challenging on occasions. The Top Bants team reckons this chapter is a bit boring but we all agree, very important for a comfortable life.

Get a doctor/dentist

Being healthy is one of the most important parts of being a student, regular health, dental health, mental health (and not forgetting sexual health).

Doctors (for those who live in the UK know), are a nightmare to get an appointment with. Often it can take weeks, and by which time, you're usually well again.

Dentists also have a horrendously long waiting list - so be aware!

TOP BANTS TOP TIP

Sign up for a Doctor and, if possible, an NHS dentist ON ARRIVAL at university. You can call them a few weeks in advance to organise a date to go to them to register. MAKE SURE YOU DO THIS!

In the event that you are sick and your doctor can't see you, call the NHS Direct phone number and speak to a professional. If you have a severe health issue then go to a local NHS walk in clinic or emergency room.

First Aid

So, at some time you're going to need a plaster for that new shoe that rubs, that sports injury, or that trip down the stairs you didn't realise about until the next morning. It's really handy to know a bit of first aid to;

- to treat yourself or a friend
- to save you time
- to save you money
- to ensure you don't have to take time out of lectures to get professional treatment
- to keep the parents happy!

Your first aid pack should include the following

- Something to clean a wound, in liquid form (TCP is great - yes we know it stings) but you could use any cheap pour on or spray on antiseptic liquid. Cheapest is currently available in pretty much every pound shop and has a long shelf life! If you have nothing to hand use boiled water with some salt in it. Allow it to cool and clean the wound.
- Something to cover a wound. Again, all top supermarkets have long bands of plasters that you can cut to size and come out much cheaper than individual plasters. If you're used themed plasters from home, get creative, draw on them before you pop them on to the wound!
- Something for a sore bite or spot. (we're not talking bites to the necks from Freshers here, but more insect bites) Top Bants recommend an aspirin, crumbled between two spoons and then mixed with boiled water to a paste that you can put on these bites to get the sting out.

Diabetic, epileptic, asthmatic or nut allergy?

You'll be a super worry to your parents. Who have cared for your illness, and ensured all meds are on hand throughout your life. You will have the bases covered we know but, that won't stop them worrying. The Top Bants team have had quite a bit of experience of this and, trust us, the better you are organised with this stuff the safer everyone around you will feel and there will be less hassle and worried questions asking you, have you done this, got that etc..

TOP BANTS TOP TIP

Ensure your new friends know of your condition. Don't be ashamed to tell them if you have any of the above, but more importantly, TELL THEM where your medication is, in case of emergency. We suggest you keep it beside your bed. Even though, you know what it is, pop up a big sign just like the one we have produced for you on the next page!

ICE
In Case of Emergency

Allergies

MEDICATION

Emergency telephone numbers

This will enable your close friends to locate it quickly, and also to be able to inform emergency services in the event that something goes wrong!

<u>Freshers week / fortnight / month and Freshers Flu</u>

Without exception the entire Top Bants team has suffered from Freshers Flu. Why? We work hard and play hard and, frankly we're simply members of the 90% who get it and can't work out how the 10 % avoid it! If you discover the secret… let us know how! #topbants

Homesickness

Even though none of us like to admit it, in retrospect and after a long lunch, every member of the team confessed to being home sick in one form or another! Here a few ideas that help;

- Make yourself super busy with extracurricular activities. Sports, specialist associations, debating, Christian society, knitting clubs, chess clubs, or simply student socializing.
- Its fine to phone home and it's actually OK to phone home a lot! But if it makes you super sad, message home and explain, and perhaps text daily but limit calls to once or twice a week.
- Get a few recipes from home. There's space on the following page for someone to write things.
- Write a letter to home. There's nothing better than receiving a letter, and not enough people send them these days. You never know, you may even get one back!

- Talk to friends, you'll find they're going through a similar thing, and they may be grateful for the chance to open up to someone.

Remember, being home sick is normal; you miss your comfort, family and friends. Time helps with this and if you can keep yourself busy, give yourself time this will get less and less difficult.

Why Freshers Flu?

So imagine all of the germs in the entire world, gathered together in one small area (your university/your halls/your lecture theatre). So many Freshers, not to mention older students, will have been away for their summer holidays and over the course of summer have contracted some kind of bug that they very readily pass on with their return. You're mingling with all of these germs, hugging your new classmates, kissing them, touching the same door handles, grabbing the same trays, trying each other's drinks at the endless streams of Freshers parties and those pesky little germs are flying from one person to another infecting every unsuspecting student as they go!

TOP BANTS TOP TIP

Don't go out, don't see anyone, don't go to lectures, don't share drinks, and don't hold door handles, or touch anything anyone else has touched! OK let's be reasonable - Under no circumstances is that going to happen.

Don't share drinks or try someone else's, if you bite into someone else's pizza, remember they've been touching it already, and even if you bite from the other side to avoid catching those germs, you're going to be biting into any germs they have on their hands, so GET YOUR OWN PIZZA.

#dontbelikestephen!

Make sure your hands are clean! There's no need to go over the top with this, but using alcohol rub (most chemists sell it for under £1) is a good start. We're not going to suggest you don't hug or kiss your new uni mates, let's face it, you want to join in and integrate in uni life... it's going to happen!

Freshers sleep... or lack of it!

All of a sudden there are no parents to pick you up, there are parties that go on in to the early hours of the morning and somehow with all of this, you have to get up and out of bed and attend lectures and Freshers events. The experts recommend getting as much sleep as and when you can. Like that's going to happen! But as it's what the experts recommend we feel an obligation to pass this on!

Alcohol

Nothing like stating the obvious! But yes, Alcohol in excess is most definitely going to compromise your immune system. It will affect your judgment, so you will most likely eat that piece of half chewed pizza you're offered.

Are you a drunken hugger? Oh bring that on... get hugged loads and pass around those germs!

TOP BANTS TOP TIP

We feel a responsibility to advise against drinking alcohol (there you go… we said it). One member of the Top Bants advice team from Nottingham University has never touched a drop! Yet she's the life and soul of the party and also a great friend to have if you need a lift home or a sober person to talk to! YOU TOO could be that sober person

Junk food

Now we know (because we've been there) that your junk food resources will deplete significantly in week one. #dontbelikestephen. How about hiding them from yourself and rationing these so that by the end of the first month you'll still have treats in the cupboard!? NO?

Try to supplement your diet with effervescent vitamin tablets (always ensure you dilute these in water otherwise you'll walk around like a rabid dog i.e. foaming from the mouth).

Pop to the supermarket and capitalise on their reduced fruit section. Think fast food, handy, cheap and healthy!

Sexual health

We can't stress enough the importance of your sexual health. You know the dangers, but just a quick set of facts here to encourage you to keep your pants firmly on. #dontbelikestephen

If you have slept with two people and each of those two people has slept with two people you have indirectly had sex with 126 people. There's a "sexual calculator" online. We just lied and said we'd slept with 2, but then, we played with this a bit more (because we had nothing better to do) and the statistics are horrifying.

Please also remember, that anal and oral sex ALSO COUNT!

You can catch the most horrific life changing STD's from casual sex and even if you know of your partners sexual history, do you know of their previous partners sexual history? We don't need to go on, but suggest you Google "super gonorrhea" and look at the images.

Next time you're considering a casual sexual encounter you may want to think twice.

TOP BANTS TOP TIP

There are heaps of people milling around campus with free condoms in Freshers week, and there are many resources you will be informed of to enable you to get free condoms, collect as many as you can! Even if you don't want them, you can be "That friend" who has some! Remember please they have an expiry date!

So university feels relatively safe, and indeed, in the main, it offers a wonderful transition from home life to independent life. We don't want you to be scared, but we do need you to be realistic and we base this word of caution on our own experiences. Here are a few points that we know you know but …

- Make sure if you go out at night you have a good bunch of solid friends or at least friends who live in your accommodation. Ensure you have each other's phone numbers and can find each other on messenger apps.

- Agree to stick together… no matter what.

- Agree that if one member of your group is going on somewhere else that they will call you to let you know they're safe.

- Agree to walk home together and the route you'll take.

- Agree a time you aim to get home and attempt to stick to it!

- There's nothing uglier than a really drunk person chundering in the street. Don't be that person! #dontbelikestephen

- Watch out for your drink. You all know the dangers of having drinks spiked and one of our team has inadvertently experienced that. He was fortunately with a bunch of friends who could protect him and get him back to the safety of his home. It can happen to anyone. Don't leave your drinks unattended.

- Drink where possible from a protected bottle. Watch out for your friends drinks too.

- Don't phone mum and dad at 4 am to tell them you love them. They know this already. Don't use your mobile phone to text your ex to tell him or her you still love them, remember the reasons why they're your ex.

- Do text your parents to tell them you're home (if that's what you have agreed)

- Do text the friends you've been out with to tell them you're home safely (again, if that's what you have agreed)

- ICE - In Case of Emergency? We mentioned this on pages 130 -131. How about having this as your home screen on your phone? Also share your ICE contacts with your closest new buddies and get them to do the same! You never know when you could need emergency contacts, and it's great to know that your friend has a contact back home too if necessary.

Chapter 11

Random Bants

Getting a part time job

We have to be realistic and accept the fact that you're most likely destined to live in poverty for the next few years however; there are some great part time jobs out there that you can either apply for or indeed create for yourself. We appreciate that some full time degrees mean you're too tired from lectures and revision, but there are so many ways, you can get through university with a small job.

Benefits of a job;

- You get to meet people outside of your uni friendship group
- You have more money
- You appear enterprising to any future employer
- It looks great on your CV
- You reduce the amount you have to borrow on a student loan that will need to be paid back later!

Applying for a job

Double check your CV, ensure it's up to date with your university status and updated contact information on it. Apply through agencies, direct to the organization, ask your new uni friends if they know of any work going and look on the student information boards. There are lots of people who look for part time employees for, bar work, waitressing, seasonal work, shelf stacking, marketing or sales campaigns, to cover a shortfall in staff. There are often jobs at the university, so ask around.

Creating a job

Oh my goodness, the Top Bants team is great when it comes to creativity! We've put up adverts for babysitting, applied for dog and house sitting positions nearby! We've made and sold fancy dress costumes (James has bought fancy dress costumes)! We've done dog walking, we've fed cats, we've cleared gardens, and we've even offered our services as cleaners! Some of them have frankly been pretty horrific, but some have been a great way to earn some extra cash whilst having fun.

One of our team found stuff for free on local advertising sites, picked it up, cleaned it off and sold it to make a tidy profit! Others have fixed peoples computers!

Remember, not all of this work needs to be for a financial exchange. Exchange your services and abilities with others, offer to cook for others if they buy the ingredients and have some fun whilst doing things you like!

Updating Mum and Dad / Guardians and Friends at home.

Remember them! Well you wouldn't be where you are today if it wasn't for them! (Not forgetting, of course, a great deal of hard work on your behalf). For the last 18 or so years, they have gone out of their way to help you, feed you, protect you from the world and grow you into the awesome human being you are today!

They don't want to bug you but, we guarantee they're sat at home wondering what you're up to and visiting what social media you have allowed them to access to see that you're OK. We know you don't want to be bugged by them but, they only do it because they love you and miss you so much - and they care!

Take time to message mum and dad (don't forget your siblings too). Take time to call or agree a good time to call home each week, it will be the absolute highlight of their week to hear from you!

Don't forget to sign off with an "I love you" or a "thank you x" every now and again!

Don't just call parents, guardians, and friends when you NEED them!

Kebab shops - go when you're sober

Top Bants story!

There was this one kebab shop we'd visit every night on the way home from clubbing! We'd either catch a cab home, or walk up Park Street in Bristol and get a kebab with the money we'd saved.

This was until one particular night, when I went in sober - never again! That awesome kebab place, with the lovely guys who'd give me extra meat, was a grotty hell hole, full of germs, and how it passed its hygiene inspections we'll never know!

Doing free stuff and advice from the team

James   OMG, you don't even think about the free stuff, until you have no money! I joined the gay running club, great way to meet new people, and make friends.

Hannah   I was really lucky, but then I'm used to being poor, I found it was fun going for picnics in parks, visits to museums, and applying for tickets to random gigs through social media got me into some free clubs, and concerts. I even got free tickets to the theatre! Keep your eyes peeled for offers, and giveaways on local social media sites!

Emma   I'm pretty busy with my social life to be honest, but glad I joined the hockey team, as we have loads of free events, and also free visiting lecture evenings with free pizza from the sponsor!

Stephen I find I meet the most random of people and seem to get invited back to there's for a nightcap. There was this one occasion when I met a wine expert, a whole crowd of us went back to his house for free wine. I puked everywhere and then the unimaginable happened, when I had a small accident in the bathroom. I didn't know what to do with my boxers so I hid them in the toilet cistern! …we are not able to print more of this story!

Make notes here of free things to do, and make sure you check off one new thing each week! #dontbelikestephen and wait until your finals to get to know your university city.

FREE EVENTS AND ACTIVITIES

FREE THINGS & PLACES TO GO!

No Spend Day

OK so this is fun, even better if you can have deliberate no spend weeks! And even more fun, when you can go without buying stuff, knowing you're saving the money you'd spend at a party for the weekend!

The fact is, that every time you go to a supermarket you're always tempted by stuff you really don't need and of course that odd bar of chocolate or can of your favourite drink. All these extras add up and, over the course of the year, can save you a fortune, if you avoid them in the first place.

Imagine, you visit the supermarket 3 times a week. Each time you buy a little something extra for £1. That's £156 you spend on extras each year!

Aim to reduce your supermarket visits to once a week. Go with a list of essentials, but always remember to check the reduced isle. Remember, you can always freeze items you find on the day you bought them and use them the following week.

TOP BANTS TOP TIP

Take cash with you, and leave your card at home, this way you'll stick to a budget!

Remember - no spend... also includes online purchases (don't cheat here).

Borrowing money is one of the worst things you can do, it's time to discipline yourself, and work to a budget!

If you want to make a purchase, question;

- Do I need this?
- Can I find this second hand?
- Do my parents, friends, grandparents or siblings, have one they no longer need?
- Can I borrow this item?
- Could I sell on this item again?
- Finally, ask yourself again if you REALLY need this item!

If it's not urgent sleep on the idea overnight, and ask yourself again the next morning if you REALLY need this! If the answer is yes, then, and only then do you need to make this purchase.

SAVING MORE MONEY!

TOP BANTS TOP TIP

Never take your card on a night out.

James	Oh yes, I did this, I can't even remember if it was a great night out, I was poor for the entire term - school boy error. Yes James…
Bethan	Oh yes, I did a similar thing, only my card was stolen, never again.
Emma	Nope never! I learnt not to do this before I started uni!

Taxis

Always use a recognised taxi company, only use one that you have booked and never ever ever take a taxi that pulls up and offers you a ride in the street - they could be anyone!

James	I always walk home.
Hannah	Yes to be fair, after a night out I always walk home with friends.
Bethan	Can't afford them.
Emma	Uni gave me the contact of a good taxi company, I actually did have to call them once when I was stuck on the other side of town, I keep details of taxi companies recommended by uni. Make sure you get into the one you've booked.
Stephen	#dontbelikestephen

Rail cards/Travel cards

If you're doing any travelling whatsoever, we strongly suggest you look into budgeting for travel cards. Look on your uni website, and visit webpages listing travel card deals for students, you can get some stonking offers.

Always remember to take your student card with you when you sign up.

Banking

Online/high-street, the world is your oyster and coming up to September you'll find all banks advertising for special student rates. Some offer you money to open an account with them; others offer a great array of discount vouchers.

Watch out for deals on credit cards and attempt to never go into your credit limit, as you will be charged a fortune in interest. If you do inadvertently spend money on a credit card always pay it back in full at the end of the month.

Sign up for deals

Thank goodness for social media hey! We (the Top Bants team) love a great deal. 2 for 1's, ½ price for students, 75% off! Student nights, Buy one, get one free, it's an advertisers dream out there!

Remember though, it's only a deal if it's something you NEED!

Do you seriously need 3 large tubs of cappuccino mix? Do you NEED the free burger with your "go large meal" (James says he does)! Would you buy it if it was full price or do you just fancy it? 75% off, now there's a bargain, but do you seriously need 10 years supply of A4 paper and an industrial stapler? #dontbelikestephen

Do your admin

It's a nightmare that we even have this title within the book, because we're all pretty useless when doing our own admin. If you have uni emails, make sure you read them and deal with them straight away.

If uni are demanding bits of paperwork, then just get it over and done with and send them!

If you have to apply for a student loan or some travel documentation, don't leave it and sit on it, JDI as Hannah would say "Just Do It".

Don't lock yourself out

James has just confessed to at least four occasions when he's locked himself out of student accommodation. Many of you have access codes and cards now, but if you have a key just get another one cut and swap spare keys with a reliable friend. It will save you a fortune, not forgetting the time and inconvenience of it all, OR INDEED the humility James suffered going to lectures the next day in the same clothes he'd partied in the night before!

Gaining space in your fridge - fridge politics, cupboard politics, bathroom politics

OOh here's a biggie and some views from the team.

Emma	I want to be in my accommodation two days before everyone else so that I can block off enough space in the cupboards and fridge for my stuff.
Hannah	Doesn't care because to quote her "it will all be ok in the end".
Stephen	Just uses everyone else's stuff. That may explain where the chocolate muffin has gone from the editor's fridge. #dontbelikestephen
James	Is the only one with wise words to share on this occasion, so we'll go with James!

"Let's face it, there's never enough space in the cupboards or the fridge. I tended to keep a lot of my stuff in a box in my room. About a week into non-catered halls, we had an impromptu powwow over hangovers in the kitchen. It didn't get heated, mainly because we were still all trying to establish our friend groups. We agreed on rules, and space. We agreed to tidy up after ourselves and from time to time, someone would blow a gasket or leave a note. The worst thing is when people don't wash up after themselves, but again, a bit of naming and shaming soon sorted that out!"

Stephen   "Yes I stole your chocolate muffin... I also drank your coconut water."
Says it all! If it's precious, special, or a treat... just don't leave it out for the Stephens of this world!

Insurance

You'll need to check with your university and the admin team that manage your halls, as to which insurances you need, and perhaps discuss with your parents regarding what items need insuring.

TOP BANTS TOP TIP

Often your parents will be able to get their personal home insurance to cover you. Check with them, explain it will save a fortune, and hopefully their insurance company will cover you too, without the need for taking out an extra policy!

Make friends in advance on social media

Join groups, create #hashtags and work your magic. The great thing about social media is that even the shyest student can start to make virtual friends.

Stephen says "Be careful with group messenger" He won't tell us why, but we suspect some significant faux pas in the past, that he's too ashamed to talk about!

Stephen also recommends removing your location settings from all apps. Not only do you want to end up with your own personal stalker, but Stephens experience lost him one of the first serious dates he's ever had!

Find your phone

We did a quick hands up around the table. Who's lost their phone? The answer, yes, all of us! Oops! Let that be a quick lesson to all of us, and you too!

Stephen	has lost his a whopping 7 times. Two of them were brand new iPhones.
Bethan	confesses to dropping hers down the loo and fishing it out again (still working -EUCK). Even Hannah lost her brand new Samsung on a night out, and now has her brothers old phone.
Emma	has "mislaid" her phone so she says (could be interesting to track it and see where).

So… With this in mind,

- Go online and download the "find my phone" app. It's free and works on all phones as far as we know. Ensure you remember your setup and password.
- Ask the parents/or check with your provider to see if it's insured.

- Or finally - get an old phone... the older the better and stick with this! You'll save a heap of cash and no-one will want to steal it!

Get a bag for life

We're all about recycling - even James! Save money on carrier bags, and save the planet, by borrowing a few "bags for life" from home!

> TOP BANTS TOP TIP
>
> Get two identical bags. This way, when you have heaps of food shopping to get, your body is balanced when carrying the stuff home and you won't hurt your back!

Games to learn before uni

OK so - as every student knows, you NEED to have a cool collection of card games up your sleeve for those occasions when;

- You run out of things to say.
- You can't be bothered to chat bants.
- You're at a party which needs some mojo injected into it.
- You're predrinking.
- You're bored.
- You want a competitive game.
- You're on public transport.
- You're in a park, with no money, but need something to do with a bunch of friends.
- You have no money to go out, but have a bunch of friends to entertain.

- You have heaps of friends in the same penniless state as you who need entertaining.
- You're looking for an activity to bring a group of new friends together.
- You can't think of any magic tricks or jokes to liven up the evening.

Card games are THE BEST! All you need is a small pack of cards (visit a pound shop or the nearest supermarket) and away to go - you have hours of fun and entertainment at your fingertips!

Here is just a small selection of some of our favourites, but be sure to contact us with your own recommendations or when you put a new spin to the game! #topbants

Paralyser

One of the simplest set of rules to remember, though, pretty much guaranteed that by round two, the rules will slip.

You'll need a minimum of four players, a deck of cards, and about as much alcohol as you can muster.

The dealer lays 2 x 8 rows of cards face down on the table. And then deals two cards to each player (including the dealer) These cards can be seen by all players.

The line of cards closest to the dealer is the "Take a drink row", and the line of cards furthest from the dealer is the "Give a drink row". Ready…

Dealer turns over the card on their far left in the row closest to them.

Any player with a matching card plays their turn card one, means take ONE drink.

Dealer turns over the card on their far left in the row furthest from them.

Any player with a matching card nominates someone else to take ONE drink.

On to round two.

Dealer turns over the next card on the left in the row closest to them.

Any player with a matching card, plays their turn card two means TWO drinks (and so on)

Dealer turns over the next card on the left in the row furthest from them.

Any player with a matching card nominates TWO drinks. These can be donated to the same person or given to two separate people, i.e. one drink each and so on.

The third card in each line means three drinks…etc…

Ring of fire

Gather a group of friends, a glass each, a deck of cards, and some alcohol.

You'll need a clear table space. Arrange the shuffled cards in a circle around the table.

Categorise each card, for example

1 - Waterfall - Everyone must drink until the person who picked the card stops.

2 - Choose - you can choose someone to drink.

3 - Me - You must drink.

4 - Paw - Do your favourite animal impression.

5 - Pretty sure you've got the idea of this, so keep the ideas coming!

Beer Pong

One of our favorite games. Known also in our office as Wine Pong, Champ Pong, and Tequila Pong. Depending on the nationalities playing, you may need to agree on the rules before you start!

You need a Ping-Pong ball, a table, two teams of people and some glasses, mugs or cups filled with your favourite drink. No Ping-Pong ball?

Don't worry, at a push you can use a rolled up ball of paper wrapped in sticky tape, or a piece of foil.

Set up an even number of glasses at opposite ends of the table in a triangle shape. Each team stands at opposite ends of the table beside the glasses and lobs the ping pong ball into the opposing team's glasses.

Once a ball lands in a glass, the opponent drinks the contents of the cup which is then moved from the table.

The winning team is the team with the most glasses / mugs / cups left on the table.

TOP BANTS TOP TIP

Have a cup of water to wash the ball if it falls on the floor!

Drinking Jenga

For the uninitiated, Jenga is probably one of the easiest games of all times. It revolves around a stack of 54 wooden blocks, though if you're anything like us, we now have 51, as Stephen lost 2 under the fridge, and one other is missing, possibly, also under the fridge!

The blocks usually come in a perfect shaped box, with four blocks to a row, that you can slide out (if put away correctly) and start your game.

Going around the table, each player has to take away a block from the stack until elements of the stack (or indeed the entire stack) fall down.

Of course, over the years, the blocks have been painted on or written on with an array of forfeits, anything from simply having to down a drink, or play the rest of the game with your socks and shoes off. So, if you have a trusty family game of Jenga at home, grab it next time you're back, doodle on the bricks with a load of forfeits, and voila... you have your own personalised version of Jenga!

PS – Hannah says you can find Jenga in pretty much every charity shop these days!

Stephen also has a lot of recommendations for drinking games, one of his favourites including the song Jolene. #dontbelikestephen

Inspire other students and tag us. #topbants

Chapter 12

Random Bants

The Top Bants team is an eclectic mix of intelligence, madness and social animals. During the process of writing this book we sat, we chatted, we drank beer, tasted wine, and brainstormed each and every element of this book. To give you the most honest and up to the moment account of what university life truly entails.

A great deal of subjects discussed at the table ended up as one long chat that started with "There was that time that…" and had us roaring with laughter by the end. We debated if we should share these personal cock ups in this book, and then agreed, that yes, just a few fun ones could go in at the end, and so… (A bit like the outtakes of a film) here they are!

What did you pack?

So we brainstormed a list of suggestions of things they did or didn't pack for uni, what they used, what they never used, what they thought was ridiculous, and items they thought were imperative (especially for your first year) we thought we'd list them, with our experience to enable you to make your mind up!

Scissors

James   Oh God, what an error, used them to cut a sticky up bit of hair before a night out. An experience not to be repeated!

	In retrospect, this was a really silly idea. Did I use scissors other than that? No I never found them again, and just used my teeth to open things.
Hannah	F*** yes, of course you need scissors! They're great for making fancy dress, I cut some chain men and coloured them in and hung them across my room for decoration… I was that person who lent them out to friends, and demanded them back within the hour, I couldn't do without my scissors, also useful for jammed paper in my printer, and a screwdriver on my drawer.
NOTE;	If you're going to shove scissors in your printer, ensure it's turned off at the mains and the scissors are removed before you turn it back on again.

Sewing kit

| Emma | WTF, I'd not know how to use it, do people really need a sewing kit? |
| Hannah | Er yes… again, fancy dress, sewing on buttons, and also to use the needle to clean the mud out of the earphone jack on my phone, oh also you can use the pins to open your mobile phone drawers for your sim! |

Sharp knife

| Stephen | Don't know if I have one! #dontbelikestephen |
| James | Oh how unprepared was I! Erm, I did have a blunt knife, like a butter knife, wish I'd thought of a sharp knife now. |

Emma	Got a sharp knife, well, it's not so sharp, but it was, it can cut apples and stuff but slips off when I cut onions.
Hannah	Sharp knife, and when I go home, I take it with me to get it sharpened… how do you guys live without a sharp knife?

Baking tray

Stephen	What?
James	Erm? (Says it all James).
Hannah	Yes! You can cook just about everything on it, including cookies.
Emma	You what? Oh like to put on that wire thing in the oven? … No!

Alarm clock

James	No - got my phone
Hannah	Yes but what happens when you run out of battery? … And yes, I have one
James	Then I'm late.
Emma	Got a 2 meter phone charger from a pound shop.

Laundry basket

Emma	No - got an Ikea bag.
James	I just scrape everything from the floor and shove it into a plastic bag if I can't reuse it.
Hannah	God you lot are awful! Ok, so I have three, one for coloureds, one for whites, and a small one I take to the launderette with either whites or coloureds in it. I prespray stains with a stain remover before I go, to save me carrying the bottle.

Photos of friends, animals and family

Emma   No - I have them on my phone.
James   My family made me a mug with the photos on it.
Hannah   Yes, I have a collage on my wall (Good job she
            took her scissors with her).
Stephen   Nah, all the photos are on Facebook anyway!

Dressing gown

Hannah   Yes, a towel type one for after my shower, and a
            kimono for hanging around the halls.
Emma   Yes but I've lost the belt.
James   Yes Batman.
Stephen   Er... Boxers? #dontbelikestephen

Big thick blanket

Hannah   Yes, handy for snuggling up without getting into
            bed.
Emma   Hell yes, wrap it around me at my desk, my
            room is freezing.
James   I've got a sleeping bag.
Stephen   Duvet (man of many words).

Emergency stash of cash

James   Always use my card.
Hannah   Yes, I have it in my piggy bank.
Emma   I check my pockets and usually find the odd
            amount in there, best day was when I found £5
            in my winter jacket.
Stephen   I've exhausted all my emergency cash.
James   Yes, and he owes me a tenner!

4 way extension lead

Hannah	No.
Emma	No.
James	Yes for my PlayStation.

A plant

Hannah	Yes, I have two, a spider plant, and a basil plant named Basil.
Emma	Had a cactus because you don't have to water it.
Hannah	Yes Emma, you DO have to water it.
Emma	Had it for two years... oh perhaps its dead!
James	Resounding no.

Bin

Hannah	Yes.
Emma	Yes.
James	Did have, but had to use it for some game, don't know where it's gone, so I have a poly bag on the back of the door handle.
Stephen	Did you lot all really have this stuff? #dontbelikestephen

Decorations - fairy lights

James	What?
Emma	Yes - pink hearts, over the bed.
Hannah	Don't think we're allowed them in halls.
Stephen	Yes.
Hannah	WTF?
Stephen	Yes, I've got snowman ones up.
Hannah	But its July.
Stephen	But they're lights!

Pillows

Resounding yes from all

2 metre phone charger

James	No, but have a power bank.
Hannah	No, 2 meters isn't that excessive.
Emma	Not if your bed is the other side of the room and you need to charge your phone.
Hannah	Can't you charge it at the other side of the room?
Emma	No then I can't check my messages in the night.
James	Flight mode all night, I don't want to fry my brain.
Hannah	I'm with you James, I'd never keep it next to my bed.
Emma	Why? (Says it all Emma)

Clothes hangers

James	No. I don't have a wardrobe, oh hang on, I got one free with a jacket that I hang up on the door, but no, I didn't pack one.
Emma	Yes.
Hannah	Of course - saves on ironing.
Stephen	Huh?

Duvet covers / pillow cases

James	Yes, Thomas the Tank.
Emma	That's lame James.
Hannah	That's pretty cool actually, yes, mine is, pink and has unicorns on it.
Stephen	No.

Door wedge

James	Why?
Hannah	So you can keep your door open when you first move in.
Emma,	I just shoved my chair in the way.
Hannah	I took one, and used it loads.
James	You could use a bit of cardboard and save money to be fair.

Swimming kit

James	Yes, super handy, as I can wear my trunks as boxers when I run out of clean undies.
Hannah	James, you're gross.
Emma	Good idea to be fair.
Hannah	Actually we should go swimming.
Emma	Have you seen this hair when it's wet?
Stephen	Yes, I go swimming. (WTF Stephen).

Joggers

Resounding yes from the team.

Keyring

James	That would have been a good idea.
Emma	Yes, with my name on it, Christmas prezzie from my brother.
Hannah	That's a stupid idea, if someone found it, they'd know who you are and be able to break into your room.
Emma	I find it's handy when I forget my name LOL.

Sleeping bag

Yes from all.

Squash / Cordial

Emma	Yes good for adding to cheap vodka.
Hannah	Yes, love it hot when I have a sore throat or I'm bored with coffee.
James	No.
Stephen	Yes, I don't drink tea or coffee.

Bin bags

James	Er.
Emma	Yes, good for taking the dirty washing home.
Hannah	Yes, and for putting your rubbish in.
James	Yes but think about the environment (We fear James has never considered this).

Sandwich bags

Hannah	I use a sandwich box.
Emma	Yes me too, well a sandwich box.
James	Erm (We think James is tired of this game)
Stephen	No, I eat my sandwiches before I leave, or reuse crisp packets.
Hannah	But what about lunch.
Stephen	I don't really leave the house before lunchtime. #dontbelikestephen

Ethernet cable

James	Of course.
Emma	Er…
Hannah	Yes, but never use it

Headphones

Resounding yes from all except Stephen, who didn't pack his, but seems to be in possession of James' headphones.

USB stick

Again, yes from all.

Chargers

Of course.

<u>Social media imprint</u>

This one caused a big debate!

Beth	And so there was that time that I stalked my stalker.
Hannah	Huh?
Beth	Yes, he had some unpronounceable name, and was from some unpronounceable place, and told me he wanted to marry me.
Erin	You know you should just block these people right.
Beth	HA HA yes, but it was so much fun. I fed him all these lines about how I was going to his country, and about how attracted I was to him.
Erin	What on earth…

Beth	Well I didn't give him any personal information, and blocked him from seeing everything on my page except my photo (which was of the dog) and yet he still went on and on about how pretty I was. I kept it going for weeks, he was robbed and lost all of his money just at the point that he was coming to see me in the UK, then he started asking me to lend him money to get here.
Hannah	WTF... you didn't.
Beth	No... ok so first off, I have no money, secondly, he had none of my information, and thirdly, I had absolutely no intention of seeing him. But more to the point, I thought, that at least if he's busy chatting me up, then he wouldn't be bothering anyone else! So I told him I was coming out to find him, asked him all about his family, asked his address, he sent me heaps of photos including one of his penis, which was just gross, I'm guessing he found it on Google.
Erin	BETH!
Beth	Yup, I kept him chatting literally for weeks.
Hannah	Then what.
Beth	I got bored, I actually realised I was probably chatting to about 10 different people sat in some dodgy office somewhere, and in the end I couldn't be bothered to play their game, so I blocked him.

MORAL OF THE STORY - Don't engage with scammers in the first place. Beth was lucky, and a bit silly, as you just don't know what other information is out there online about you.

Just for the bants we went stalking to see what we could find.

Before our Social Media chat, we went off stalking our teams photo's to find some incriminating evidence, that you really don't want your future friends or employers to know about or see.

- An ill-considered political rant about Trump with an inappropriate photo. Go careful with these things, you never know when you need a visa, green card, or are even offered a job as an intern in the White House (one of our team was).

- A rant about Brexit, and the "lower classes". It became a real classist debate! This doesn't reflect the Top Bants member we know and love and so we asked her why. Apparently, it was done late one Friday night to wind-up some friends... This has since been deleted BUT IT'S OUT THERE SOMEWHERE!

- A repost from a far right group. This Top Bants member hadn't even considered what the post was about, but just wanted to share the photo to show her mum, because the house she grew up in was on the image!

- An anti-gay comment from a member of the Top Bants team who is gay!? OOhhh dear! It wasn't terribly offensive, and as he says, it was most likely shared during his "denial period".

TOP BANTS TOP TIP

Go through every social media you have ever used, check,
check and check again. Check comments, check photos you've
shared, and a bit like clearing out your wardrobe of those
clothes you thought were cool three years ago… clear out the
debris.

Weird house-mate experiences and funny ones too.

James	So we were having this party one night, and one couple ended up together in the bathroom. Anyway, the next morning we noticed the sink had come off of the wall.
Erin	Classic party at your house then!
James	We didn't want to tell the landlord cause it would cost a fortune, so we just pushed it back into place.
Emma	Fair.
James	Yes, but the trouble was that every time we used the sink it leaked into the downstairs flat, so finally we called the landlord. The day before he came, I pushed it back into place again, but there was all this white type glue around where it had been. We tried to think of ways to make it look like it had never come off of the wall, then I had a brain wave to put some of this white stuff around the sink again to make it look like nothing had happened, only, I couldn't find any locally, and he was coming that day. So one of my flat mates suggested we could use toothpaste… MASTER PLAN!
Emma	Oh my God I have this vision…

James	So the landlord came and the bathroom smelt of toothpaste and as he checked out the sink, all the toothpaste got stuck to his hands.

TEAM CRACKS UP

James	So yeah, he made us pay to fix it we'd only been in the house for a few weeks.
James	So then there was that time when I woke up in the middle of winter to find my bedroom window wide open and the car park barrier half in my bedroom and half hanging out of the window.
Erin	WHAT?
Stephen	Oh yes, I did that.
Everyone	WHAT?
Stephen	Yes, it was some truth or dare thing, and I had to run out and get an item from the car park, and I couldn't get a car up the stairs, so I unhooked the car park barrier and we carried it up.
James	STEPHEN... I got into serious shit for that!
Stephen	Ha, sorry about that, to be fair, it wasn't an easy mission and the only way we could get it into your room was by opening the window.
James	You bastard.
	Ha... but then there was that time it was Stephens's birthday and I got him that frog fountain.
Stephen	Oh yeah, I actually loved that.
James	You know it's an antique?
Stephen	Mmmm and ...
James	Found it next to some bins just up the road!

The Top Bants team got on to the cooking section of this book.

Emma helped us significantly here, as she was useless in the kitchen, some of our favourite comments include;

- "What's a colander?"
- "Oh that's garlic, I never knew it was an actual thing"
- "What, you put eggs in a cake? I HATE eggs!
- "Is eggplant eggs?"

Whilst practicing making the mug cake;

Emma	OK so this cake is just like sugar and chocolate and oil.
Erin	Did you put the flour in Emma?
Emma	Oh no, that's why it's like sugar and chocolate and oil then!

Whilst practicing making the mug cake, take two.

Emma	Ok its gone hard at the bottom and it's more like a cookie than a cake.
Erin	Did you use this self-raising flour?
Emma	No just the plain flour from the box.

Whilst practicing making the mug cake, take three

Emma	Oh nooooo it's gone everywhere!
Erin	Ok what happened?
Emma	I doubled the recipe so we'd have two to photograph for our social media.
Erin	But you've only put it all in one mug.
Emma	Yes, I realise that now.

Photo of the chocolate cake on Instagram isn't so pretty, but that was her final attempt!

Opening a wine bottle without a corkscrew.

Stephen	So we could give advice on how to open a bottle of wine without a corkscrew.
Erin	Not sure that's a clever idea Stephen.
Stephen	Ah no, to be fair, I did end up in hospital when I did it
James	WTF… of course you did.
Stephen	Well we'd gone out for a picnic, and I was trying to be romantic like, so I went to open the wine, and realised it wasn't a screw top. Then I remembered some survival guide I watched where they opened one with a shoelace and a flip flop or something. Anyway the top smashed off and I cut my wrist and hand pretty badly, and had to get stitches.

Emma learning how to use a wok;

Emma	So could you stir fry just about anything?
Erin	Yes, but if you're using meat and stuff, you need to ensure it's cut thin, and well cooked so that you don't get food poisoning.
Emma	So could I stir fry chips?
Erin	Oh God Emma.
Emma	Yes but can I.
Erin	Well yes… you could Emma.
Emma	Ah see, I can be creative.

Top Bants team brainstorming

How to feed yourself cheaply

Stephen	Oh I had a couple of occasions when I nailed that.
Erin	Oh cool Stephen, go on I'll note them down.
Stephen	Well one day, I just walked into the kitchen and there was spaghetti bolognaise already cooked in the pan on the hob.
Erin	How do you mean already cooked?
Stephen	Well it was just there and cooked.
Emma	What so you just took it?
Stephen	Well not all of it, I left some for them.
James	WTF… it was YOU?
Stephen	Mmmm, it was good to be fair.
James	I don't believe it, you bastard!
Stephen	Also…
Emma	Oh God.
Stephen	Well some good advice would be to date people in the campus canteen.
Erin	Stephen… what, REALLY?
Stephen	Well yes, it all started really with just a bit of flirting, and getting extra chips and stuff…
James	Stephen, you're just such a tart.
Stephen	But then, I'd hang around, and when it was getting to the end of the food service, I'd just pop up and give her a cheeky smile, and get the leftovers.
Erin	You are actually such a tart.
Stephen	Yes, but I took it a bit too far.
James	Oh God
Stephen	Well I asked her if she'd like to come for dinner, and… well OK so …CENSORED"
James	And so you didn't go back.

Stephen	Oh yes, but then I had to flirt with her mate instead, and then…No, we can't use that one in the book either, it really didn't work out, but it was free food!
James	Go on.
Stephen	Well when I was super poor, I got a job in the pub next to uni just clearing plates and loading the dishwasher but on the second night I went out to clear this table and this lady hadn't eaten her chips so as I went to take the plate, I bent down to grab a handful and as I walked away with the plate, I dipped one in the bowl of tartar sauce on the table. #dontbelikestephen
Erin	What the hell were you thinking Stephen!
Stephen	What, chips without Tartar sauce?
Emma	That's definitely not going in the book, let's move on.

Whilst talking about personal safety

Erin	Anyone else had experiences they want to share
Kim	Well then there was that time I actually lost my life in Freshers week.
Emma	Your life?
Kim	Yes, literally everything! You have to remember this was my first real time in London, it was Freshers week, and I somehow had my purse stolen. Lost my keys, my passport, my visa card, my money, my phone… like EVERYTHING
Erin	We don't want to frighten our students.
Kim	Yes, but it's easily done, and we should warn them.
Erin	Ok so perhaps we should have a section on, 'When you lose your life?'

James	Bit drastic to be fair - not everyone is as air headed as Beth.
Stephen	I am.
Erin	Yes but you don't count. So Beth, if you could pass on one piece of advice to our readers to avoid losing their life… what would it be?
Kim	Never take your card out in the first place. Take student ID and not your passport. Keep your phone in your bra…"
Erin	No don't keep your phone in your bra, you don't know what the radio waves will do to you.
Hannah	No, I'd not keep it in my bra.
Erin	OK how about put it on flight mode when it's in your bra?
James	Is there honestly any great advice to avoid losing your life, pretty sure we've all lost elements of this?
Stephen	How about, stay aware when you're out and about, and make sure you don't take your eye off the ball, James, don't get so shit faced that you cannot remember half the night hey… JAAAAAMES!

Top Bants team turn to stare at Stephen who has offered the most useful piece of advice in this whole process! Stephen does have his uses.

Stephen	With safety, how appropriate is it for us to talk about sex, because safe sex is so important!
Emma	Yes, super important, though you'd like to think the students know about it. Oh and super gonorrhea, I saw a great photo of this the other day, you can even catch this through oral sex.
Hannah	Well of course you can, you can catch heaps of stuff through oral sex.

James	Nooooo.
Hannah	FFS James… please don't tell me you don't know about this. What about hepatitis?
James	But not oral sex!
Erin	This needs to go in, because if James thinks this… then imagine how many other people think oral sex is safe.
James	Shit, please don't let my mother read this book!

Weird housemates

James	How about a section on how to handle weird housemates?
Erin	Oh yes, we've all had weird housemates!
James	I had one that stole my bath once.
Emma	What? Like, took it?
James	No, I had a rugby injury and needed to soak my back. Got my Lush bath bomb, ran a super deep bath, then I'd forgotten my towel. I was only gone a few minutes, went back and someone was in there, I waited a bit, then went back to my room and my phone rang. I was gone for about five minutes, got back to the bathroom to find my bath was horrid and grimy, and the person who'd used it had even taken the plug out, there was this massive grime stain all around the bath.
Stephen	Yes, that may have been me, I smelt gorgeous though…

The rest of this conversation is censored! #dontbelikestephen

Pranks and all that stuff

Stephen	How about a section on pranks?
Erin	No Stephen.
Stephen	But they're so much fun and we could do it as a "be warned" type section.
Everyone	No Stephen.
Stephen	But the prawn and cheese pranks?
James	No that was just gross Stephen, it stunk the entire floor out for weeks, and anyway, was it an actual prank, or did you just forget you'd put the cheese behind the radiator to get it to room temperature?

A resounding NO TO PRANKS from the Top Bants team!

Whilst talking about stains…

Emma	Ketchup stains, like… never come out.
Erin	Sounds like you're talking from experience there Emma.
Emma	Well yes, bit of a ketchup fight in halls, and then amongst our housemates in second year.
Erin	Do we think it's appropriate to include this?
Stephen	Well yes, who doesn't have a ketchup fight?
Erin	But how responsible is this?
Stephen	How responsible are students?
Erin	Yes but we need to reassure parents that their kids are going to be responsible young people.
Stephen	Yes but this is uni we're talking about, and we have a duty to cover all angles.
Erin	OK Emma, so what did you do when the ketchup went up the walls?

Emma	Well one time it happened, I just left the party, and left the boys to clean it up as they'd done it in the first place... but the other time, it was an F'ing nightmare, it landed on the wood chip wall paper, it was pretty grim to be honest, and we tried literally everything to get it off, only, it just ended up pulling the wallpaper off"
Erin	So what would that top tip be for this situation?
Emma	Put a mirror on the wall to cover the torn wallpaper.
James	Or, don't have ketchup fights?

Dealing with vomit

Erin	So we need to talk about vomit, because even if our readers are sensible, they'll have friends who are sick, and chunder stains are a nightmare!
Hannah	Yes, but how do we cover every type of vom stain - do we categorise them? It will take ages!
Emma	We could talk about where to chunder.
Erin	Yes, but there will still be accidents, so I think we need to cover this.
Hannah	Erin, sounds to me like you're talking from experience here.
Erin	Well yes. I did once go to a housewarming party with a friend. It was in a super posh area of London and the apartment was like the inside of an interior design magazine. We'd had some heavy pre's and, actually, didn't envisage we'd end up at the party. I was probably the youngest there and it was the night I was put off Tequila for life.

Stephen	Oh Erin!
Erin	OK Stephen, so I'm not perfect. I was literally sitting in the chair, and all of a sudden, I just puked from nowhere it was like projectile, and all over their brand new cream carpet.
James	Ha ha - what did you do.
Erin	What do you think? I left... really quickly!
Hannah	And the stain?
Erin	Pretty sure they never got it out... so we can't put that in the book then.
Emma	Chunks, we should have a section on chunks.
Hannah	Chunks?
Emma	Yes chunder chunks - you know... the bits of carrot you always find in your vom.
Hannah	Ok so on a scale of 1 - 10 how appropriate would this be?
Emma	It happens, even after a dodgy kebab, it doesn't necessarily have to be drink related.
Stephen	True.
James	So what's your advice to our readers Emma, chew their food better so there are no chunks?
Emma	No but understand me here, if you can catch the chunks in some kind of colander thing then you have less mess to clear up.
Stephen	You only found out what a colander was today Emma!
Emma	Yes, and I'm going to have one in my kitchen now all the time, especially to catch chunks.
Erin	I'm not sure this conversation is getting us anywhere to be honest.
Hannah	I caught my vom in a hoodie once.
James	WTF?
Hannah	Yup, on a bus. I just had to throw up, and I couldn't get off the bus, so I took my hoodie off and caught it in there.

Stephen	To be fair, we could list places to chunder into... I was sick in one of James' saucepans once.
James	WHAT?
Stephen	It didn't have any food in it!
James	Well that makes it fine then - please tell me you washed it out.
Stephen	I popped it in the sink if that's what you mean.

TOP BANTS TOP TIP

Don't hang out with the Top Bants team! They're brutally honest, and pretty gross to be around sometimes! #dontbelikestephen

When discussing the launderette;

Stephen	We really should put a warning about leaving your clothes in the launderette and going to the pub.
Erin	Sorry?
Stephen	Well there was this one time, when I was leaving for Tenerife the next morning, and I had to get all my washing done and dried, cause I literally had no clean clothes.
James	Go on.
Stephen	So I popped the clean stuff in the dryer, and then went to the student union for a drink. Somehow I forgot the time, and when I went back the launderette was closed, and all my clothes were locked inside.
James	Ha ha, I've not heard that one, so what did you do?
Stephen	I went back to the union to finish my beer.
James	But what about your clean clothes for your holiday?

Stephen	Just had to cut off the bottom of my trousers and turn them into shorts.
James	Not sure any other student in the world would be so bloody disorganized.
Erin	So that's not going in the book then... moving on.

We'd like to thank each and every member of the Top Bants team for their hilarious and outstanding contribution to this book. For the hours of banter, the broken mugs, the scratched frying pans (thanks Emma) and above all else, for being awesome students!

We know you'll have the most awesome experience at uni, so do please share your adventures with us!

Tag us on social media, we're always looking for new inspiration, and will be there to console you on your failures in the kitchen, and in fact, through your student life! #topbants #dontbelikestephen

Visit our YouTube channel for inspiration #topbants

One final note, a reflection perhaps, or simply a motto for life.

"If it's not fun... don't do it"

and above all else...

#dontbelikestephen!

Index to recipes;

For further information and inspiration, join us on Facebook Top Bants or find us on Instagram #top_bants_clean_pants

Printed in Great Britain
by Amazon